CARING FOR CREATION

CARING FOR CREATION

A CHRISTIAN WAY FORWARD

by

Chris C. Park

Marshall Pickering
An Imprint of HarperCollins*Publishers*

Marshall Pickering
An Imprint of HarperCollinsReligious
Part of HarperCollins*Publishers*
77–85 Fulham Palace Road,
Hammersmith, London W6 8JB

Published by Marshall Pickering 1991
9 8 7 6 5 4 32 1

© 1992 Chris Park

The author asserts the moral right to
be identified as the author of this work

A catalogue record for this book
is available at the British Library

Phototypeset by Intype, London
Printed in Great Britain by
HarperCollinsManufacturing Glasgow

For Samuel James Park

CONTENTS

CARING FOR CREATION

ACKNOWLEDGEMENTS

Like my other books, I have written this one because I could not find within one cover any attempts to explore the themes which appear here. Just like before, I set about the task of writing the book that I had hoped to find someone else had already done! Inevitably I have learned a great deal in the process, and I have emerged with more questions than I originally started with! But en route I have been able to sort out my own ideas and (hopefully) fit them into a framework which comfortably accommodates what many others have written.

That such a lengthy task could have been completed so quickly, so enjoyably and so effortlessly is witness to the grace and love of God, the creator and sustainer who rightly plays the lead part in this whole story. My prayer is that you will see something of God's power, majesty and care through reading and thinking about the material within the book, and that you will pardon any errors I have made in my enthusiasm to tie so many different threads together.

My debt to the Lord is obvious both to me and to those who have seen my life change in so many wonderful ways in recent years. People have played a key part in that, too, and I am indebted to my family (particularly my parents) and friends for making my life such a happy and productive one. My special friends at my spiritual base, St Thomas' Church in Lancaster, have been an endless source of love and encouragement, and I trust that Robin and Jill Bundy, Steve and Audrey Potter, Cyril and Muriel Ashton, and Peter John and Anne Davies realize how much they mean to me. Cyril deserves special mention, both as Vicar at St T's and a trusted friend, for encouraging me to write the book, suggesting Marshall Pickering as a possible publisher and offering helpful suggestions on the text. Christine Whitell at Marshall Pickering helped me to carve the text out of my overlong manuscript!

My immediate family have tolerated the writing of this book with customary ambivalence! Angela, my closest friend, harshest critic and wife, understood what this book means to me and was more generous in freeing me from family duties to create time for reading, thinking and writing than I could ever have asked for. She may even read the finished product! Our beautiful daughter Elizabeth Ann was born while I was pulling material together and before I started the serious writing; she is a never-ending source of joy. Her brother Samuel James never ceases to amaze us, and believes that everybody's Daddy writes books all day long! I dedicate this book to him, with the prayer that – like his namesake in the Bible – he will continue "to grow in stature and in favour with the Lord and with men" (1 Samuel 2:26).

PART ONE

GREEN PROBLEMS
AND
ATTITUDES

CHAPTER ONE

THE ENVIRONMENTAL CRISIS

It is now two decades since Hugh Montefiore, then Bishop of Birmingham, writing on the theological issues raised by the ecological crisis, concluded that "what is needed is . . . a redirection of inward attitudes".[1] He concluded that this might perhaps best be achieved through a better awareness of our responsibility as stewards of God's creation.

Since then four important developments have made his conclusions even more relevant to today. A series of major environmental disasters (like the North African droughts of the 70s and 80s, the explosion at the pesticides factory in Bhopal in India in 1984, the nuclear accident at Chernobyl in 1986, and the mounting problems of air pollution by greenhouse gases) have deepened the so-called "environmental crisis". Moreover the "crisis" has evolved and broadened, incorporating some other leading social issues of the day, into the wider "green debate". Third, the general public has woken up to the possible environmental impacts of their own actions; we now understand that it is *our* problem, not someone else's. But in addition Christians around the world have started to reflect on where they stand – and, moreover, where they *should* stand – in all this.

Yet, perhaps surprisingly, the central theme of our responsibility as stewards of God's creation is still relatively unexplored and poorly understood. I hope in this book to try and establish some of the boundaries of the green or environmental debate, to chart the main relevant themes (in their historic and contemporary contexts), and to offer a starting point for a balanced biblical understanding of our role as stewards. If nothing more, I hope to offer the basis of a Christian perspective on the debate.

Christians *should* have a genuine concern for the state of the world, but we should be cautious about accepting the whole package of green thinking without first searching through the scriptures and establishing clearly where we stand as followers of Christ. We should keep in our minds two important questions—

(i) what does it mean to be green? and
(ii) how compatible is it with being a Christian? In other words, can you be green and still be a Christian, and vice versa. Both groups (Christians and greens) often claim that they have the right way and the other is at fault. But they are compatible, up to a point.

What does it mean to be green?

The label "green" is now used to mean environment-friendly or environmentally aware.[2] A "green" person, in today's use of the term, is someone who cares about what their lifestyle does to the environment, and cares enough to change those things which seriously affect the environment. This is why they probably drive a car which uses lead-free petrol, use recycled paper, take used aluminium cans for recycling, buy organic foodstuffs, and so on.

Greens are concerned about the health of people as well as the health of the planet. There is, today, a complete package of green practices which embrace all aspects of lifestyle and livelihood. It is *not*, in its pure form, a convenient add-on to our normal lives, or a shallow cosmetic pursuit. To be truly green demands total commitment.

To be green is not only acceptable today, it is fashionable. Because of that, it is marketable. Think of all those adverts in magazines, trying to persuade you to buy products like ecologically-sound washing materials, recycled paper products and bleach-free disposable nappies.

People are green for all sorts of reasons. Some, the "hippy" greens [3], are determined to reject the conspicuous and wasteful consumption of modern society, and opt to go "back to the land", buy clothes second-hand and live a sustainable, environment-friendly alternative lifestyle. There are even families living full time, year-long, in Indian teepees in central Wales ... going to extreme lengths to escape from "the rat race".

No doubt many people are green today because it is fashionable. This group has been labelled the "style-conscious yuppie environmentalists"[4]. They tend to value goods that last a long time and are good investments. Classically designed clothes in natural materials, which are expensive but long-lasting, are *de rigueur*. High-quality arts and crafts which reflect creativity of artisans and require little material and energy are also highly prized.

But green does not simply mean environmental, with which no thoughtful Christian could take serious offence. It goes much further and wider than that to embrace a whole kaleidoscope of aspects of lifestyle, livelihood and attitude, including broader issues of resource use, economics and politics. Some of them Christians might accept, possibly for different reasons; but others the two sides (greens and Christians) would doubtless part company over.

The green movement has many faces, and it is starting

to influence our lives in a variety of ways, whether or not we consciously try to be green as individuals. Green politics surfaced for the first time in Britain in a serious and effective way in the 1988 Euro-elections, since when the big three parties (Conservative, Labour and Liberal Democrat) have tried to be greener than each other in their statements if not their policies. Even Margaret Thatcher, then Prime Minister, had her own green "road to Damascus" experience in November 1988. Even if the Green Party itself has extremely limited electoral success, the popularity of green issues has guaranteed that the main parties have quickly jumped on the passing green bandwagon.

Green consumerism is also big business, and many high street stores are selling many different types of green products. Consumer habits reflect lifestyle and aspirations, both of which are starting to have decidedly green tinges to them for many people.

Environmental problems are very practical issues, but beneath the surface are some really significant spiritual questions, and the emergence of a new green spirituality is one of the most interesting features of recent years. Green spirituality is, for the first time, being taken seriously by all the major world religions.

Jonathan Porritt, former Director of Friends of the Earth, has been a charismatic spokesman for the UK green movement through the 1980s.[5] He was well placed, therefore, to conclude in 1988 that "things are moving fast. Green ideas have moved decisively from the fringes of society, which they occupied less than ten years ago, into the mainstream ... green thinking has already had a considerable impact on the way we live".[6]

Shades of green

Many people have in practice been green for years, probably without realizing it! Using recycled paper, picking up litter in the town and countryside, wearing clothes made of natural rather than man-made fibres are in themselves green things to do . . . but the list *can* go much further than that!

One of the most complete checklists of criteria for being green is offered by Jonathan Porritt in his book *Seeing Green*[7], one of the first popular books on the subject. He regards the following as a minimum list of criteria—

- a reverence for the earth and all its creatures
- a willingness to share the earth's wealth among all its peoples
- prosperity to be achieved through sustainable alternatives to the rat race of economic growth
- lasting security to be achieved through non-nuclear defence strategies and considerably reduced arms spending
- a rejection of materialism and the destructive values of industrialism
- a recognition of the rights of future generations in our use of all resources
- an emphasis on socially useful, personally rewarding work, enhanced by human-scale technology
- protection of the environment as a precondition of a healthy society
- an emphasis on personal growth and spiritual development
- respect for the gentler side of human nature
- open, participatory democracy at every level of society

- recognition of the crucial importance of significant reductions in population levels
- harmony between people of every race, colour and creed
- a non-nuclear, low-energy strategy, based on conservation, greater efficiency and renewable sources
- an emphasis on self-reliance and decentralized communities.

This is a formidable list, from the pen of a leading proponent. Clearly not every green person would agree that this is a perfect list (with nothing important left out, or nothing irrelevant put in), nor would they all rank each goal as of equal importance . . . but the basic framework is generally agreed. Many of these sound Christian, or at least are not in conflict with the fundamental Christian values of love, humility, respect for others, concern for the poor and the oppressed.

Measured against Jonathan Porritt's rather daunting definition of the set of beliefs which "very green" people are supposed to hold, it is clear that some of us are greener than others! This is perhaps inevitable, given that people turn green from different backgrounds, and with different motives. The green movement is not a single body, nor does it have a single philosophy or world-view. It spans a spectrum of interests, and encompasses a variety of views and goals.

Greens can – and indeed do – occupy most shades along the traditional colour spectrum of party politics[8]. At the blue-green end are those people who have an old traditional conservative outlook. They believe that nature sets limits to human aspirations so that we should respect the primacy of the "laws of ecology". Blue-greens try to preserve what is left of natural resources and traditional landscapes. At the other end of the political rainbow are the red-greens. These people (often socialists and Marxists at heart) stress that nature and natural things are basically social constructs created by world-views and social relationships that are deeply rooted in the material economic organization of society. They favour progressive ecological change coupled with radical social reforms and radical (if not revolutionary) change in political and economic organizations. The middle-ground of green politics is occupied by the green-greens, who claim to be radical and new but in reality promote a mixture of ideas drawn from left and right.

The point is this – there are lots of different ways of looking at the world, even within the green movement. Unless, as Christians, we are prepared to recognize that alternative world-views to our own exist, that many of them have some validity, and that some may have important things to offer us, we will only get a selective glimpse of what it means to be green, and only have a partial and partisan understanding of today's green movement.

What's gone wrong?

For at least the last twenty years scientists and journalists have been talking about an "environmental crisis", by which they mean that we are damaging the environment so much that the situation is now critical.

Few people doubt that the world is in a mess, the mess is getting worse, and we are responsible for both! Mankind seems to be the only species which knowingly continues to foul its own nest, when it already has a fair idea of what damage it is causing. We spoil the earth every day and in a million ways, such as chopping down tropical rain forests, overfishing the oceans, dumping toxic wastes on land and sea, and polluting the skies with acid rain and nuclear fallout. The checklist would be enormous, and it would implicate just about every aspect of so-called civilized living which we tend to take for granted. We pollute land, air and water; we over-use valuable natural resources, supplies of which diminish and prices rise; we exploit wildlife in ways which are not sustainable, so that species after species becomes endangered or extinct; we create waste products which are harmful to people and wildlife.

There is no shortage of evidence that things are going badly wrong, and that we are destroying the world's environment on which our health, livelihood and very survival depend. Whilst it would be out-of-place to examine the key problems in detail here, we ought perhaps to think briefly about some of them [9].

Air pollution, mainly by invisible gases, is produced mainly from factories, houses, power stations and vehicle exhausts. This material can be blown by the wind over vast areas, and can damage human health as well as wildlife. An estimated 625 million people worldwide live in areas (mainly industrial cities) where the air is unhealthy. By 1986 acid rain had caused visible damage to over a third of the forests in six European countries. Increased levels of ozone in the lower atmosphere decreases crop yields in the United States by up to 10% and damages lung and respiratory tissues in humans. At the same time ozone depletion in the upper atmosphere (caused mainly by CFCs, or chlorofluorocarbons) is allowing more incoming harmful ultraviolet radiation from the sun to reach the earth's surface, threatening to increase the incidence of skin cancers and cataracts in humans. Air pollution by greenhouse gases (including carbon dioxide, nitrous oxide and methane) is already starting to cause global warming, and scientists predict that average global temperature will rise by 1.5–4.5°C by the year 2030 – causing patterns of temperature and precipitation to change significantly, and sea levels to rise.

One of the most serious environmental problems today is the continued destruction of tropical rainforests and woodlands. These are being cleared at a rate of around 110,000 km² a year (equivalent to an area the size of England in just over 14 months); four-fifths of the forest area is cleared for farming and the rest is selectively logged. Although the tropical forests cover only about 6 per cent of the world's land surface, they are an essential part of our life-support system. They help to regulate climate, protect soils from erosion, and provide habitats for millions of species of plants and animals (up to nine-tenths of all the species of wildlife on earth live in the tropical forests).

Beyond the tropics, many species of plants and animals are under threat because their natural habitats are being destroyed. Other wildlife is threatened by excessive hunting and trapping for trade (especially species which are rare and endangered, like rhinos and African elephants). The oceans are being over-fished (catches rose from about 30 million tonnes in 1958 to 90 million tonnes in 1986), putting at risk sustainable yields of some species. Pollution of the oceans is also reducing fish harvests in many areas.

Another critical part of the equation is population pressure. There are simply too many people expecting too much of the earth's environment and resources. And the numbers continue to grow. World population doubled between 1950 and 1987, reaching 5,000 million. Two more people are added to the world total every second!

Reliable estimates predict a further 1,000 million by 1998, and by 2025 the United Nations predict a global population of 8,200 million (with nine-tenths of the growth concentrated in the developing world).

But it is not just the total number of people which matter, it is their distribution ... especially in relation to access to resources. The 26 per cent of the world's population who live in the developed world consume 80 per cent of the commercially produced energy, up to 86 per cent of the metals and up to 34 per cent of the food[10]. Little wonder, therefore, that serious inequalities exist in health, wealth and quality of life between developed and developing countries. Scientists believe that enough food is grown each year to feed the world's 5 billion people, but there is widespread hunger mainly because of inequitable distribution of land and wealth. A fifth of the world's population (950 million) are permanently hungry, and many of them live in South Asia and Africa where population growth rates are particularly high.

We could examine other ingredients of the environmental crisis, such as the growing use of chemicals in intensive farming (and the allied risks of pesticide poisoning), or the problems posed by disposing safely of the estimated 325–375 million tonnes of hazardous waste created world-wide each year. But to do so would only reinforce the conclusion that we are seriously over-exploiting and damaging the environment, and we are putting at risk the ultimate sources of our food supply and raw materials (the forests, fisheries, farmland and so on).

Historic context
Whilst scientists have written at length in recent years of the environmental crisis, there is nothing new about

the idea that mankind is damaging his environment. Many of the ideas, concepts can be traced back through earlier writers, and there is abundant evidence from earlier periods of human history that people have exploited or mismanaged their environment. For example, it is known that forest clearance is a traditional form of land management which has been carried out throughout the settled world for at least the last 4,000 years. Forests have been felled in present-day Sahara and Arabia since 5,000 BC, in China since 2,000 BC and in the United States since about 1800 AD[11].

Human activities have caused the extinction of wildlife through the millennia. For example, many large American mammals (including mammoths and many species of horses) became extinct towards the close of the last Ice Age, possibly because early Americans used fire drives to encourage whole herds of big game over cliffs for hunting[12].

Air pollution is not new, either. Appalling conditions in seventeenth-century London are described by John Evelyn in his 1661 book called *Fumifugium, or the Smoake of London Dissipated* – "whilst these (chimneys) are belching forth their sooty jaws, the city of London resembles the face rather of Mount Etna . . . or the suburbs of hell, than an assembly of rational creatures, and the Imperial seat of our Incomparable Monarch"[13].

Just as there have been serious environmental problems through the ages, so there have also been prophets of doom through the ages. Yi Fu Tuan, an American geographer, has studied how many old cultures like the ancient Egyptians, the old Chinese dynasties and the Aztecs in South America share "a persistent lack of confidence in the cosmos as a going concern". But he goes on to say that "people have always known food shortages and famines, but they usually confronted them as present realities in this or that place, not as a world-wide catastrophe yet to come. The global scale and the future tense are thus new."[14]

The journalists' maxim that "bad news is good news" applies well to much writing about the environment, and there is no shortage of gloomy pessimists eager to explain just how nigh the end of the world now is! Some of the self-styled prophets of ecological doom have relied on shaky quasi-scientific arguments, whilst others are simply plain old sentimentalists who prefer a rustic past to a high-tech present.

There have been plenty of scare stories before – the early 70s in particular was an era of gloom and doom environmental writing. For example, scientists from the Massachusetts Institute of Technology wrote a report in 1974 which predicted what might happen in the future if recent trends (in pollution, resource use, population increase and so on) were allowed to continue unchecked[15]. They forecast a point within the next century when serious shortages of natural resources will lead to falling industrial growth, limited food supplies and a marked drop in the human population caused by pollution, famine, disease and stress.

Critics of this pessimism school – and there are plenty – point out that despite such bleak forecasts of impending doom we are still here! "Just how sound is the argument?" ask the optimists, as they conclude that the prophets of doom invariably insist that the worst will almost inevitably happen. The pessimists always seem to blow the issue out of all proportion and overstate the case, and they do so with insubstantial, incomplete and often inaccurate data, insist the optimists.

This debate between positive-thinkers and negative-thinkers – the optimists and pessimists – is more than just academic, because recently the pessimists' case has been attracting most of the attention in the media. This is one reason for the rise of popular interest in green issues . . . it reflects fear in the future survival of the earth and its life-support systems. But is this fear justified?

Many people are convinced that there is plenty of good news to indicate that things are improving, and they conclude that talk about an environmental "crisis" is indefensible scaremongering. Certainly there are encouraging signs. Many industries, for example, are investing heavily in efforts to develop and introduce new production technologies, choose alternative materials, and treat wastes so as to reduce if not eliminate harmful effects to people and environment. A wide range of economic and political measures is being introduced in different countries to encourage the use of environmentally-sound technologies. Demands for the introduction and enforcement of tougher standards of pollution control continue to rise, and campaigning groups (like Friends of the Earth and Greenpeace) are raising awareness and mobilizing citizen-concern for the environment.

So . . . what's new?

Many people ask, "Is the situation really as critical as some people are saying it is?". There are problems, of course, but is it really a *crisis*? The answer depends partly on what we mean by the term "crisis".

Optimists say, "There have been environmental scare stories before, and we are still here – so who is kidding who?". But such an argument overlooks several important aspects of today's crisis which make it quite different from past situations.

One is the global scale of damage. We now have the

power to change the environment on a global scale, for the first time ever. Many of today's pressing problems are affecting the whole world. For example, if the hole in the atmosphere's ozone layer continues to grow, then people around the world will suffer from excessive amounts of damaging ultraviolet radiation; or if felling of tropical rain forests continues, we will all be affected by the resultant climatic changes. Many environmental problems – especially air and water pollution – are international, because they cross national frontiers. Recall how far the nuclear fallout from Chernobyl was spread (certainly right across Europe, within a week), and think of the export of acid rain from some countries (like Britain) which is quickly imported elsewhere (like Scandinavia). Serious political as well as scientific problems are posed by such uncontrollable movements.

A second new cause for concern is the speed with which serious problems are building up. Rates of change are getting faster. In a typical day some 30,000 hectares of tropical forest (an area roughly the size of the Isle of Wight) is destroyed or badly damaged; deserts advance over a similar area; some 200 million tonnes of valuable topsoil are washed or blown away, one more species becomes extinct and 100,000 people (nearly half of them children) die from starvation[16]. Imagine how big these figures grow over even a month, let alone a year.

The long-lasting effects of many environmental problems aggravate the situation ever further, and it means that we are passing on to future generations problems which we have created but for which we have no solutions. Some of our waste products, such as toxic chemicals and radioactive wastes from nuclear power stations, will still be around in thousands of years' time. Today's land-use changes, such as forest felling and the building of cities, might trigger climatic changes which affect the next century or even further ahead. Activities which cause the extinction of wildlife species have a cost which stretches to eternity, because extinction is forever.

Many scientists are worried that we are now stretching ecological systems to their breaking point (critical thresholds beyond which irreversible changes can occur). This makes the present situation more serious and more critical than ever before, and it means that the options available to generations which follow us (including our own children) will depend largely on what actions we take. The planet has a finite ability to absorb our wastes and renew its resources, and to knowingly approach those natural limits is to deliberately play Russian Roulette with our environmental life-support system. Norwegian Prime Minister Mrs Gro Brundtland chaired the World Commission on Environment and Development, which concluded[17] that "Nature is bountiful but it is also fragile and finely balanced. There are thresholds that cannot be crossed without endangering the basic integrity of the system. Today we are close to many of those thresholds."

Another cause for concern is growing awareness that we simply don't know how many of our actions are affecting the environment and through that affecting people's health. There are many uncertainties in linking observed effects with possible or suspected causes. Think of the widespread controversy and anxiety surrounding the suspected links between leukaemia and radiation pollution, for example, or the uncertainties over what caused the seal deaths in the North Sea in 1988, or whether BSE in cattle ('mad cow disease') can be transmitted to people. New risks are being created every day, through the development of new technologies (such as genetic engineering) or the careless use of existing ones (such as the 1984 explosion at the Bhopal pesticide factory).

So, there is much that is new in today's so-called environmental crisis and there are plenty of reasons why we should be concerned about the state of the world around us.

CHAPTER TWO

ATTITUDES, VALUES AND MOTIVES

Most greens argue that the environmental debate is not just about practical issues, it runs much deeper than that and centres on our attitude and values. Why do we view things the way we do? Why do we behave as we do?

There is little to be gained here from compiling a check-list of all that we are doing wrong to the environment. The examples in Chapter 1 speak for themselves, and there is no shortage of books which show in graphic detail the sorts of damage which are now appearing. Besides, as we have already noted, problems such as global warming, air pollution and forest clearance are *symptoms* of a much deeper crisis... they are not the *causes*.

Neither is this the place to lay down a blueprint of how we should live our lives, what we should buy, how much we should buy, what we should do with wastes and so on. That is not to say that it is not important to think carefully about whether to use products like lead-free petrol, environment-friendly washing materials and recycled paper. But there are plenty of guides to green living available now [1]. What is important is to note that lifestyle reflects underlying values and attitudes, and these are the root of the problem.

The environmental crisis is as much a crisis of values

and motives as a crisis of science and damage. The root problem is our attitudes and expectations. We react according to what we understand and think, not according to how things really are. So the way we see the world shapes the way we react to it. We tend to look upon the earth as a free commodity, a limitless reservoir of resources, and a bottomless rubbish dump. Yet, at the same time, we expect it to meet all our needs with minimal cost – we expect it to be life-supporting, useful and beautiful . . . all at the same time. Perhaps this is a naively optimistic hope.

Myths and misconceptions

Two particular myths often underlie the way we view the world around us. One is the "myth of superabundance" – the idea that nature is a rich and limitless storehouse of natural resources (such as energy, raw materials and wildlife) which we can use as, how, where and when we decide . . . and it will never run out. Thus we often have very unrealistic expectations about issues like the productivity of farmland and forests, the sustainability of ocean fish stocks, the availability of new land for development. Yet the notion is deceptive (because it encourages ruthless exploitation rather than careful conservation), as well as incompatible with what we understand about limits within nature and with the inescapable truth that the earth is finite.

This false vision of a limitless nature arises from human greed; we want to have (or convince ourselves that we *need*) more, bigger and better of everything. This attitude of accumulating an ever-growing and ever-changing amount of disposable material goods is very much a feature of twentieth-century life[2]. Modern culture glorifies *things*, especially modern and new things – like fast food, fast cars and high-tech equipment. The media promotes the image of modern, new things as good and right, thereby encouraging us to buy more, bigger, better and more modern versions of the things we already have! It quickly becomes a vicious circle, which is difficult to break unless we realize what's going on and make a conscious effort to do something about it.

Closely coupled with our consumer habits is our modern obsession with material wealth and the status, prestige and power which (we believe) it endows us with. We tend to measure a person's status in terms of things like wealth, power, prestige or intellectual productivity. The mere *possession* of wealth is not enough, it must be displayed (hence it is sometimes referred to as "conspicuous consumption" or "galloping consumerism")[3].

A second myth, equally damaging to the environment but equally widely-held, is the assumption that people have some fundamental right to conquer and exploit nature. The myth continues that this conquest can be carried out without harming ourselves or the basic environmental systems on which our very survival depends. The examples of environmental damage we saw in Chapter 1 provide stark reminders of how human activities damage the environment which in turn affects people.

It is nothing short of arrogance to think the earth is ours to do with exactly as we please. Wildlife painter David Shepherd wrote a New Year Resolution[4] for 1989 which read – "It is high time that man, quite the most arrogant and dangerous animal, started treating this still beautiful but only world we have, with some respect. It is not ours to do with as we please and if we do not learn from this, it is at our own peril."

Our capacity to damage nature is closely linked with

new developments in science and technology, and a further widely-held myth is that "what can be done must be done". Such a view has encouraged the uncontrolled use of modern technology, with few safeguards adopted or little thought given to limiting the use of technology to where it is genuinely needed.

We will look more closely at some of the attitudes which modern science and technology have created in Chapter 3, but it is self-evident that technology is very much a double-edged sword. We have modern medicines which work miracles, and we marvel at the sight of men walking on the surface of the moon . . . but technology has also given us toxic wastes which are almost impossible to dispose of safely, it has given us nuclear weapons which in the past have posed a threat to the very survival of mankind, research and development in technology has required the investment of vast sums of money and other resources which might otherwise have been released for more humanitarian purposes.

Why do we care?

It is obvious that most people today *do* care about the environment, even if it is largely self-centred. Many of us probably can't articulate our motives very clearly; indeed, we may never have sat down to think about what drives us.

It seems that people are usually motivated in one of three ways – which have been labelled as crass self-interest, enlightened self-interest, and altruism[5].

Self-interest

People with the underlying motive of *crass* self-interest tend to view everything as a means to an end, and this end is usually their own or their group's well-being. They see nature as a commodity, and an inexhaustible one at that, which is there to be used and exchanged for their own benefit. This benefit might be financial (they might, for example, sell exotic animal skins), or it might be material (they might use natural plants as herbal medicines, or catch wild fish or animals to eat). This self-centred utilitarian view promotes the conservation of nature simply because we would be the losers if we didn't. It sees no intrinsic value in nature, or, indeed, in anything other than humans. Everything else is valued for what it can give to us or do for us.

A much less clinical motivation is *enlightened* self-interest. People who are motivated in this way go further than just seeing nature as there to be used; they have some appreciation of the many different ways in which nature can benefit us. An ability to see aesthetic values in nature releases us to be aware of the inherent beauty, symbolism and inspiration within the natural world, and to be conscious of values beyond sheer utility. A person who builds a home overlooking unspoiled natural countryside, for example, can enjoy tranquillity and beauty. Similarly, many people would be annoyed at the thought of destroying or altering places like Antarctica or the Grand Canyon in the United States, content with the prospect that they could visit them and enjoy them . . . even if they never *do* visit them. But the underlying motives are still self-centred human ones. Nature has no intrinsic value; it only has value because there are people around to appreciate it. While we do lose something when we spoil nature, what we lose is aesthetic; it is our loss, not nature's.

The utilitarian arguments are both practical and economic. For example, we rely on wild species to provide gene stocks from which to develop new products, such as the small rosy periwinkle in Madagascar which provides a drug for fighting leukaemia; this drug saves many children's lives and earns around $100 million (US) a year for the drugs industry.

There are also important ecological reasons for protecting nature, because everything (including all wildlife as well as soils, natural environmental cycles of water, gases and minerals, ocean currents and wind systems) is linked together by the "web of life". This fundamental interrelatedness of all parts of the environment (including people) also means that problems which affect one part of the environment (such as air pollution which contaminates grassland) can quickly spread – along food chains (to humans, perhaps by eating meat from sheep or cows which have eaten the grass) and through natural environmental cycles (to other places and to other parts of the same environment). For example, burning coal leads to pollution which changes climate and might affect the whole earth. So we really do live in *one* world.

Within this self-interest motivation there is also a moral line of argument, which is that we have a duty to protect nature because we also claim a right to enjoy it. Such a view is embodied in a set of principles for proper use of the environment which were agreed at the United Nations Conference on the Human Environment held in Stockholm in 1972. The first principle reads: "Man has a fundamental right to liberty, equality and satisfactory living conditions in an environment whose quality permits him to live in dignity and well-being. He has the solemn duty to protect and improve the environment for present and future generations."[6]

There are two other people-centred motives for environmental concern. One is the argument that we have a moral obligation to future generations and a duty to respect their rights (in this case by leaving an environment for them). "We do not pass this world on to them, we borrow it from them", it is argued. We have an abiding responsibility to look after this planet, because our descendants have an incontestable right to inherit an environmental estate which is as good as the one we inherited . . . if not better. We are in charge of the earth's future and we must face up to that responsibility.

The second such motive is our moral obligation to what are sometimes euphemistically termed the "underprivileged", most of whom are concentrated in developing countries. A typical US child has an impact on the environment equivalent to about 50 Indian children; at least 730 million people face food shortages, and 1.3 billion face serious shortage of safe drinking water. What prospect for their future if we in the developed countries continue to overindulge ourselves, overexploit nature and overload the environment with our overproduced wastes? With a wealthy western lifestyle comes high expectations, self-centred attitudes and damaging patterns of behaviour.

Both variants of the self-interest motive are fundamentally people-centred, or anthropocentric. Greens argue that this preoccupation with ourselves, and the total disregard for intrinsic values in nature which it breeds, is the root cause of the environmental crisis. They conclude that it is our attitudes which are at fault . . . expecting everything to be created entirely for our benefit. This, they insist, drives our aggressive exploitation of the environment and focuses our attention on immediate satisfaction at the expense of wider or longer-term goals. Nothing short of a wholesale reformation of human values is required, they conclude, and this requires us to wake up to wider issues of spirituality.

Altruism

An altruistic concern about nature is based on the premise that nature has intrinsic value. In other words, things in the natural world – the flowers and trees, the birds in the sky, water in rivers and the sea, even the clouds and rocks and mountains – have value in themselves, quite independent from any idea that they might be useful to mankind.

The altruistic motive for concern about the environmental crisis is based on what that crisis is doing to the earth and to all creatures great and small on it, rather than on how people are affected by the crisis. Philosophers have long debated the question of whether non-human things (living and non-living) have rights, so little wonder it is a contentious ingredient in the green debate. Altruism raises a number of difficult ethical dilemmas and questions concerning our use of the environment – such as "Do we have a right to destroy other forms of life?", and "What is our obligation to protect the world?".

One view is that our responsibilities range over a spectrum of what we might term "ethical levels"[7] – starting with ourselves (where what we do is guided only by what benefit we get out of it), our family and friends, the nation, and then outwards to all living people and future generations, and then plants and animals and ultimately the inorganic world – mountains, rivers and the oceans. Most people recognize some responsibilities at the lower levels (possibly to the nation or future generations), but have little appreciation of wider duties to the world around them.

But we do have duties and responsibilities concerning the environment, and these extend way beyond what is directly beneficial to people. This is the very substance of ethics; ethics do not describe how people actually behave, but how people ought to behave. An ethic is a rule for doing something that is not otherwise expedient. It might be, for example, the suggestion that whales should not be harvested to extinction (no matter whether there is evidence to show that this would harm people). An ethic is intrinsic (it may or may not be testable by scientific observation), and it is accepted or rejected on the basis of belief – those with faith in it accept the ethic and behave accordingly, those without faith in it don't.

Ethics and spirituality

A central challenge facing the green movement is the working out of a realistic environmental ethic. The usual source of ethics is religion or philosophy – where ideas of good and bad, or right and wrong, are established as standards of behaviour[8]. Interestingly, the focus of perhaps the most intense search for an environmental ethic today is religious beliefs ... even amongst greens who normally have little time for established religion in general, and for Christianity in particular.

The initiatives and efforts of theologians, philosophers and green thinkers are starting to converge on the search for an appropriate environmental ethic. Amongst the most promising areas of shared interest within this search are ideas of stewardship, based on the belief that we do not really possess the earth but have responsibilities to use it carefully and then pass it on in good condition to future generations ... to leave the earth as we would wish to find it. This is by no means a new idea, being firmly established in Old Testament practices and in New Testament models of right living.

There are two contrasting views on why we have the environmental crisis, each attributing it to radically different forces and each in turn looking for different solutions.

The secular view, much the more common, is that the environmental crisis is a *material* problem which requires a *material* solution. The material problem includes pollution, creation of wastes, overuse of resources and reliance on market forces; the only conceivable solutions, therefore, involve changes in science, technology, economics and politics (this is the mechanistic world-view described in Chapter 3).

The Christian view, indeed the broader religious view, is that the environmental crisis is a *spiritual* problem which requires a *spiritual* solution. Human sin and separation from God have given rise to the crisis (and the attitudes and values which underlie it), and the only solution is repentance and reconciliation with God. The solution is change in people.

Self-centredness and stewardship

The root problem, which has a spiritual basis but very practical consequences, is the common view that human beings are the most important things on earth, more properly described as *anthropocentrism*. This is a relatively recent attitude but it is largely taken for granted in the rich and materialistic west.

As green writer John Button points out[9] this view, taken to extreme, would argue that we own the earth, we are fully in charge of it, and we can run it just as we please. Nature is there just to serve us and to please us. It is a short step from this sort of self-centred attitude to concluding that we can use other people and resources just as we please. Hence domination, exploitation and control are justified as inevitable, as we pursue wealth and progress as individuals and collectively in society.

Such thinking raises several fundamental questions. Why was the earth created? Who owns it? Many greens argue that the earth exists for its own purposes, that nature is in control (hence the heavy emphasis on ecological principles of interdependence, cycles and rhythms of life). In its greenest form this gets translated into reverence for Mother Earth, and sometimes expresses itself in paganism, animism and nature worship.

The green debate is ultimately a spiritual debate, and one of the biggest dangers of the recent upsurge of public interest in environmental issues is that the debate has become a target for the application of New Age philosophy. We shall explore this whole issue in more detail in Chapter 3, but we should note here that an emerging blend of green and New Age ideas (such as the ecumenical but nature-centred Rainbow Covenant favoured by the World-Wide Fund for Nature) is very attractive to many people. Many of today's leading green writers borrow ideas and expressions from the New Age Movement. While this does not necessarily mean that all of them are New Agers, it does signal that New Age infiltration has been extensive and is often deeply hidden and dangerously subtle.

A number of factors have allowed this spiritual hijack and infiltration to occur, including a rather obvious failure of the Christian Church to take a firm stand in the green debate. Some denominations have recently started to launch important green initiatives (we shall examine some in the final chapter), and some Christian writers have written useful and informative books on the environment. But as yet there has been no collective response by the Church to the green debate, and individual Christians have been largely left to their own devices in deciding how, where and when to enter the debate.

Respect for people and planet, rather than exploitation, is another key feature of green belief. Many greens, concerned about the need to respect and value nature and resources in their own right, are calling for new relationships with the earth based on stewardship and trusteeship . . . rather than domination, tyrannical control and oppression (such as occurs when basic human rights are ignored).

Stewardship involves looking after something (such as land or natural resources) and taking care of it, without necessarily owning it. A trustee looks after something on behalf of its owner. The relationship is based on trust – the owner trusts his trustee to look after his possession, use it sensibly and in a sustainable manner, and be willing to give it back when the time is right.

The concept of stewardship provides a useful and traditional framework for a Christian approach to ecological issues. The world is God's creation, and he trusts each one of us to look after it on his behalf and to share it amongst everyone else . . . not to overexploit parts of it for our own gain or to accumulate wealth, power or prestige for ourselves. Looking at the world like this raises important questions of principle. For example, who decides how to share the resources out? Should he who found them have the unalienable right to appropriate them? Who should the major trustees be? How should they act?

There is also the wider question of responsibility. In many aspects of life (such as what we buy and how we travel) we can quite easily see where we personally are responsible. The real difficulties arise where we find it difficult if not impossible to say who is responsible. Take acid rain, for example. Factories and power stations pour out sulphur and nitrogen gases into the atmosphere;

vehicles emit exhaust gases; the wind blows the pollutants, they interact with other chemicals and sunlight in the atmosphere; acid rain falls many miles downwind. Who is responsible? The car drivers? The factory owners? Us . . . for buying the products made in the factory? The power station managers? You and me for wanting instant electricity, at low cost, at the flick of a switch? The Government, for its fossil-fuel based electricity policies and investments? And so on . . . we are all involved in one way or another, and in many environmental problems it is just about impossible to decide who is the guilty party. We all are; our consumer lifestyles conspire to aggravate the situation, and promote ever-rising expectations.

So, we have responsibilities towards other people and towards the earth, and our attitudes, values and lifestyles should reflect those responsibilities in fair and sustainable ways. Again, the issue centres on how we see ourselves in the global (or even cosmic) order of things. Are we all-important, or just a part? Are our rights more important than those of other people? Is our comfort and wealth more important than the survival of a rare species?

CHAPTER THREE

WORLD-VIEWS;
ROOTS AND BRANCHES

Today many people are starting seriously to question the values and beliefs which underlie and shape behaviour, both for the individual and for society at large. We have already seen how the environmental crisis reflects a dominant belief-system which tends to take for granted our reliance on capitalism, economic growth, material consumption and industrial development. But, as television sports commentator and green advocate David Icke insists in his 1990 book title, *It doesn't have to be this way*.

A brief history of changing attitudes towards nature helps us to understand how we have arrived at the present environmental crisis, and offers clues to what we might do about it. It provides us with a mental map of where different ideas come from and how they fit together. The way we see the world, our so-called "world-view", turns out to be very time-specific. If we had lived in medieval times we would have a very different attitude of mind to what we have today, for example.

Essentially the story is one of increasing human mastery and control over the world around us, as technology and culture have liberated people from being entirely dependent on what nature offered. Early man, very much an integral part of nature, had limited potential to alter his environment. Primitive tools, primitive communication and organizational skills, limited numbers in small scattered groups . . . all constrained what early man was able to do. But with developments in technology (such as the design and manufacture of farming machinery) and social organization (such as the evolution of communities and towns, and the emergence of trade and exchange systems) came an ability to extract more and more from nature of what people wanted. Gradually man grew apart from nature, no longer a part of it. We became exploiters of the natural world, and started to put fences and walls round parts of it and bring it into private ownership.

Radical changes in world-view have at times inspired and at other times been promoted by broader cultural, socio-economic, scientific and technological changes. The two often seem to be so closely tied together that it is difficult to decipher which caused which. To make some sense of the complex history of changing attitudes towards nature, we can look at three main types of world-view[1] –

1. those that centre all things around God,
2. those that centre all things around human existence, and
3. those that centre all things around the natural world.

In what follows, the term "man" is used simply to refer to people collectively. No sexism is intended.

COSMOLOGICAL WORLD-VIEWS

Cosmology is the philosophical study of the origin and nature of the universe[2], and it has traditionally shaped people's attitudes towards the world and towards nature. Four broad groups of world-view reflect an interest in cosmology – primitive mysticism, Judaism, classical antiquity and medieval Christianity.

Primitive mysticism

In this view of the world, which is pre-Christian in origin but survives in different forms in many traditional cultures, man sees himself very much at the mercy of the elements. The view dates back, in its original form, to a time perhaps up to a million years ago, before the development of stone tools and the use of fire allowed man to gain some mastery over some parts of nature and thus begin to separate from it.[3]

To early man the environment was no friend; it was hostile and had to be survived rather than enjoyed. Day-to-day survival was a relentless struggle against the cycles and extremes of natural elements like the weather, along with the unpredictability of threats and attacks from other animals and other people.

This was no cosy existence. It was man against the elements, man against nature, and man against man. Such people must have been frightened by the harshness of raw nature, yet at the same time struck by the mystery of it all.[4]

Ancient farmers who needed to combat the elements (the sun, wind, rain and fire) often had little option but to appeal to the spirits and ask them to co-operate. Thus, for example, early pagan animists made quite sure that they had placated the nature gods before they cut down even one single tree[5]. The spirit of climate or some other spirit would have to be appealed to, incessantly, in man's attempt to make the best of the difficult task of surviving if not prospering in a difficult world which seemed to offer more constraints than opportunities for people to explore.

Nature mysticism has survived down the ages in various forms, and it appears today in animism and pantheism (nature worship), as well as in some primitive religions. Shades of it also surface in the thoughts and works of the nineteenth-century Romantic writers.

Judaism

Ancient man's view of the universe was heavily influenced by natural rhythms and repeated cycles – day and night, the rise and fall of the tides, the rhythm of the seasons. His was a harmonic world. Little wonder, therefore, that his notion of time was cyclical. For him time has no beginning and no end, it just keeps going.

Our dominant world-view in the West today is very different, because we have an implicit faith in perpetual progress. We see time as directional; it is one way and irreversible, not cyclical. This view is deeply rooted in Judaism and the Old Testament, where the notions of initial creation followed by progression towards an ultimate end (the Alpha and the Omega) are fundamental and recurrent.

The Old Testament view of man's relationship with nature is one of responsibility and authority, which arises directly from the biblical story of creation as told in Genesis. God created the whole universe, including the earth and everything on it. He created them from nothing. He also created people, and gave them authority within the rest of creation to use the earth and its resources. Indeed, he went further than granting them permission – he instructed them to do so (Genesis 1:28).

But the instruction did not extend to doing anything that we want to with creation. It remains God's creation, and we remain answerable to him for our use of it. It follows logically from this that God naturally retains the right to remove that authority from us (either temporarily or permanently) if we use it unwisely, act irresponsibly, or exploit the rest of creation through greed or selfishness. Such views on authority and responsibility provide the framework for much Old Testament teaching, including views on land (which cannot be owned outright; we are to be God's stewards or caretakers, not freehold owners).

It is a conditional granting of authority, and history is full of examples of blatant abuse and self-centred exploitation. This says more about human nature than about Old Testament teaching on the use of creation.

Various writers[6] have pointed out that there is no conception of nature beyond mankind in the Old Testament, which repeatedly stresses that all creatures have the same value. For example, various Psalms describe the creation by God of mountains, waves and rocks, which in turn worship him and display his glory and grace much like people do.

The main distinction in the Old Testament is between the creator (God) and his creation (the universe, including man and nature). The emphasis is on God. Creation is portrayed as having no meaning in itself, however awe-inspiring it might be. A recurrent theme in the Old Testament is not worship of nature but of the creator and controller of it (e.g. Psalm 93).

According to the Jewish world-view, therefore, nature is valued as a reflection of God's creative power and his continued and sustaining interest in his creation. Unlike the primitive mysticism view, nature is not to be worshipped or feared. It is there to be used, as a gift from God. But it cannot be squandered or plundered; it must be used carefully and thoughtfully, and in a way that honours its creator.

Classical antiquity

The ancient Greeks and Romans saw the natural world very differently from the early Jews. To them the world was a living organism. It was animate, much like the human body, and as such it had thoughts and feelings. This classical world-view was anthropomorphic (attributing human form and behaviour to the whole natural world). Man and nature were seen as close relatives, not separate entities.

Such a view sharply influenced their attitudes and behaviour. The ancient Greeks developed very sophisticated gadgets, but they used them almost entirely for human entertainment rather than for industrial production.[7] So it might seem odd that they did not develop technology when they were obviously capable of doing so. But the Greeks did not separate nature from the rest of the universe, nor did they consider nature as an object independent from us and ready for exploration. To control and conquer nature would have been totally alien to their world-view.

The ancient Greek view of the world as a living organism was deeply rooted in their beliefs about how the world was created. As they saw it God did not actually create matter, he simply ordered it, fashioning some pre-existing disordered world into an ideal pattern (the world we see today)[8]. This divine pattern is based on a single organic whole, with mind and reason. Thus the earth is animate and nature has spirits. Every part of the universe – including nature (which consists of air, water, fire and earth), people and spirits – is a component of this perfect creature. A disturbance in one part of the unified whole (such as human disturbance of nature) could trigger a reaction elsewhere in the universal organism (such as disease in humans).

The world-view of classical antiquity saw nature as alive, highly ordered and equal in status and value to mankind. It also centred on spirits within nature, and on the need to worship and care for the natural world. It has a lasting legacy in much of today's green thinking, especially in the Gaia hypothesis (which views the earth as a living organism).

Medieval Christian

The Middle Ages span the period between the end of classical antiquity (around 476 AD) and start of the Italian Renaissance (around 1453). In Europe this period saw the flowering of Christianity, and the dominant world-view emerged from the attempt to grasp God's design or order based on a combination of knowledge and revelation.[9]

Attitudes to nature were heavily influenced by the biblical view of creation and by the Roman concept of nature as the force which directs the world (effectively, God's deputy). There was a clear shift in emphasis from the older Jewish distinction between creator and creation, to a newer Christian distinction between God and nature.[10]

A prominent development, by the early thirteenth century, was the emergence of natural theology, which was attempting to understand God's mind by discovering how his creation operates.[11] Historian of science Lynn White points out that in this medieval science "the task and reward of the scientist were to think God's thoughts after Him".[12]

But underlying this scientific and intellectual endeavour was the firm belief that man is superior to nature. Such a belief was derived from a particular interpretation of passages in Genesis which deal with man's "dominion over the fish of the sea" and other creatures (Genesis 1:26–28). Here, according to some historians and environmentalists[13], lies the root cause of our present environmental crisis. We return to this argument in Chapter 5.

But some have argued that medieval man was much more concerned about conquering himself than he was about conquering nature[14]. He saw the material world simply as a stepping stone to eternity in heaven, but one full of temptations to which he would constantly fall prey. Nature served no purpose in the overall scheme of human salvation, and there was no point even trying to conquer it. It was, if anything, a hindrance to be tolerated. The common view was that nature has no reason to exist other than to serve man.

There was not one uniform world-view across the whole of medieval Europe, of course. St Francis's life of humility and simplicity, and his recognition of all of nature as a democracy which made all of creation equally valuable and equally striking as a witness to the beauty and grace of God, provides a radically different strand of early medieval Christian thinking.

MECHANISTIC WORLD-VIEWS

The cosmological world-views reflect a belief that nature is controlled by something which is bigger than and extends beyond the limits of the universe – God or the gods. The mechanistic world-views have no need for such supernatural control; indeed, they deliberately exclude it. They view the natural world like a machine.

Renaissance and Reformation

Perhaps the most radical shift in attitudes towards nature, certainly in Western society, came during the Renaissance and the Reformation. This was a time of unprecedented cultural, social, economic and intellectual change. Nature, previously seen as a backdrop to the drama of human existence, was now viewed as a machine composed of physical parts. To understand how the parts worked was to understand how the world worked. If that could be done through careful scientific study, it was believed, God would effectively be displaced from his sovereign place as creator and sustainer of the universe.

This period was one of turmoil within the Church, and attacks from without. Never before, or since, have so many tides of new ideas ebbed and flowed with such cumulative results. Led by men of such calibre as Luther and Calvin, Bacon, Galileo and Newton, this was none other than a total revolution in western thinking which brought an attitude of domination over nature and the natural world. What was previously seen as something mystical, alive and worthy of respect and care was now viewed as something to be used, changed and exploited.

The Reformation began in 16th-century Europe, and grew from the attempt to reform the Roman Catholic Church into a wider religious and political movement which led, among other things, to the establishment of the Protestant Churches. The main leader of the Reformation was German theologian Martin Luther (1483–1546), who preached the doctrine of justification by faith not by works.

But in the context of attitudes towards nature, the leading figure was French theologian John Calvin (1509–64). He and his followers developed a new theological system which had a fundamental and enduring influence on the development of Protestant doctrine. Calvinism is based on Luther's doctrine of justification by faith, but it goes much further in its doctrine of predestination – the belief that the final salvation of some of mankind (the chosen ones, or "elect") was ordained at the beginning of time by God, and could be proven but not altered by the actions of an individual. Some have argued that this fuelled a drive towards modern capitalism and materialism which Calvinists justified by an ethic of God's calling (Calvin emphasized that individual material success is a sign of election, or God's ultimate approval).

But the sweeping intellectual changes of this era started nearly two hundred years earlier in Renaissance Europe, beginning in Italy in the 14th century. New ways of looking at, finding out about, and thinking about the world emerged with the spread of geographical discovery and the emergence of modern science. Veils of mystery surrounding human values, beliefs and potential were lifted with the emergence of modern philosophy. Classical scholarship was re-examined and its virtues re-evaluated. Secular man was emerging from the medieval era of religion and contemplation.

English philosopher Francis Bacon (1561–1626) was the founding father of modern science[15]. He rejected the science of the day which relied heavily on theory, allowed for the supernatural, had to fit in with religious dogma and didn't actually test the real world as it really is. In its place, he introduced logic and the search for answers based on experience or experiment. Bacon was interested in genuine knowledge, based on logical interpretations of undistorted evidence with a clear, rational and open mind. His legacy to modern science includes the introduction of inductive reasoning (explaining events from real world evidence) and empirical testing (devising experiments to check and re-check conclusions).

Bacon's objective study of the world opened up the opportunity for modern technology to develop, because it was rooted in the desire to understand the world as it really is, without the constraints of fanciful theories or religious conviction. Views of nature could now be liberated, and this triggered greater study, exploration and description of the wealth and diversity of the natural world. The overriding sense of mystery at the wonders of God's creation was starting to evaporate as rational scientific understanding started to increase. This trend was accelerated after Italian mathematician, astronomer and physicist Galileo Galilei (1564–1642) introduced the idea of quantifying nature, rather than simply looking at it or describing it.

Galileo looked upon the universe as a book, a great book of nature in which is written all we need to know to understand the world. The challenge, as he saw it, was to decipher the language used in the book of nature. Galileo wrote about "this grand book, the universe, which stands continually open to our gaze. But the book cannot be understood unless one first learns to comprehend the language and read the letters in which it is composed. It is written in the language of mathematics . . . without which it is humanly impossible to understand a single word of it".[16] So he developed a mathematical way of looking at the world, trying to uncover its secrets through experimental and empirical testing, measuring and expressing numerically what he saw and found.

Galileo's approach was adopted and advanced by Sir Isaac Newton (1643–1727), the English mathematician, physicist, astronomer and philosopher. Newton favoured empirical testing and quantitative studies, much like Galileo. Amongst other things, he formulated three laws of motion (or mechanics), a law of gravitation and a theory of light. He also developed calculus. To him the universe was like a huge working clock, which operated according to mechanical laws which could be discovered and described. The only acceptable forms of explanation, therefore, were mechanistic (or deterministic) ones. His challenge was to use mathematical theorems to try to discover how the world machine worked.

It follows, from Newton's logic, that what cannot be quantified (such as feelings, beauty or spiritual matters) is irrelevant to understanding the grand design of the universe. Such views, and the reasoning behind them, were summarized in his *Mathematical Principles of Natural Philosophy* (1687), although it took nearly a century for the underlying mechanistic view of the world to be widely accepted.

Whilst he was more mechanic than philosopher, Newton was not an atheist. To him God was still creator and governor of all things. He noted, for example, that "the motions which the planets now have could not spring from any natural course alone, but were impressed by an intelligent Agent".[17]

Newton was not alone, and the emerging Renaissance mechanistic world-view still allowed for creation by God. The major shift in emphasis was away from trying to understand the theological implications of the very act of creation itself, towards trying to understand the laws of nature imposed on the world by God. But the separation of God from nature implied that God was no longer in direct control. It also implied that many qualities of nature (such as beauty) only have value because we regard them as valuable (that is, they have no inherent value).

Thus emerged a dualism between man and nature, reflecting the sort of dualism which French philosopher Rene Descartes (1596–1650) identified between body and soul in people, and English philosopher Thomas Hobbes (1588–1679) identified between the individual and society. It was man against nature, not man in or with nature. Nature came to be seen as a commodity to be exploited and exchanged, and this both encouraged and was encouraged by the emerging capitalist economy in Europe. From being an object of aesthetic contemplation, nature was increasingly seen as an object of exploration, and ultimately as an object of exploitation.[18] The Renaissance context for nature and the material world was unambiguous; it was there for man to subdue, control and exploit as if he owned it. Indeed, it was mankind's destiny to do so, and was done with God's blessing.

But there were other forces at work in seventeenth-century Europe which encouraged this utilitarian view of nature.[19] Early forms of democratic government were starting to emerge. Science was developing fast, and starting to ask new questions and seek answers in new directions. Technology was evolving and new forms of production were emerging. Industrialization and progress were accepted as the norm. Humanism (belief in human ingenuity and effort rather than religion) was also on the increase, and there was an emerging emphasis on the autonomy of the individual and on people struggling to survive and improve their lot in a harsh and oppressive world.

One of the most significant forces during this period was the emergence of capitalism (the economic system based on private ownership of the means of production, distribution and exchange and the pursuit of profit under competitive conditions). Machines were starting to replace land as the primary resources for production, and human labour came to be viewed as a commodity which could be traded and exchanged. Mobile, enterprising middle-class merchants were becoming more numerous throughout Europe. Private ownership was becoming more common, bringing added security as well as tangible evidence of success. Mechanistic attitudes and capitalist values and practices were spread around the world as European traders and settlers (including Puritans, pioneers and explorers) began to colonize new areas.

We come full-circle, back to Reformation thinking, because a prime factor in the development of capitalism was Calvin's views on election (to be received into heaven after life on earth). Many Calvinists assumed that earthly success must be a blessing from God and a signal of God's approval and calling. Thus prosperity and material wealth were seen as evidence of their election and salvation. As a result Calvinists worked hard to prove to themselves and others that they were members of the elect. Personal qualities of hard work, self-discipline, frugality, honesty and sobriety were seen as virtues. The market exchange system, control of labour, generation of profit – hallmarks of capitalism – were encouraged. Although Protestantism did not *create* capitalism, Calvinism was very supportive of it.[20]

The Reformation and the Renaissance heralded the arrival of a new set of values, aspirations and attitudes. The Reformers, concerned with the souls of men, were disinterested in the idea of intrinsic values in nature. Renaissance thinking centred on man and his human potential; values were visibly anthropocentric (man-centred). The emerging new science saw nature as a vast machine, from which higher values (ultimate purpose and meaning) were excluded as irrelevant. If God played any part in the drama of human existence (and many believed he did not), it was mainly to approve of the triumph of civilization over nature like some benevolent but detached overseer.

The Industrial Revolution

Many aspects of the mechanistic world-view were to be reinforced in the Industrial Revolution. The development and diffusion of new forms of productive technology from the eighteenth century onwards encouraged and enabled more and more exploitation of nature. Natural resources like minerals, soils, water, forests, grassland and wildlife were appropriated, used, exchanged, damaged and depleted in ways and at speeds which would previously have been unthinkable.

Nature was seen as there to be dominated, exploited and conquered, all in the name of progress. Private ownership spread, along with market exchange systems and the rise of labour as a factor in production. Factories were built all over the place, in town and country, using local resources (such as timber for fuel) and producing serious pollution of land, air and water. This was the era of the "dark, satanic mills"; industrial landscapes were stark, grimy and hazardous.

Much of the blame for the environmental damage and environmentally-damaging attitudes at that time (certainly in Britain) can be attributed to the attitudes of the new breed of industrialists.[21] Before them, the land-owning aristocracy had seen themselves as the sole and rightful owners of their land. But they had also felt a keen sense of responsibility to God, their heirs and their employees. It was tradition for the family's land to be passed on down to children and their children, so land was simply held in trust and looked after by each successive generation.

But the new rising bourgeoisie – the *nouveaux riches* – had not inherited wealth from their forefathers but won it by their own hard work, enterprise and success. To them land and wealth were not gifts but prizes. As tangible signs of achievement and new-found status, their land and wealth were to be enjoyed and displayed rather than held in trust for future generations. Material goods were prized as symbols of success, so that possessiveness became a self-fulfilling prophecy. In this we might see an early manifestation of the conspicuous consumption which seems endemic in modern society. It is no accident that many of the new industrial entrepreneurs came from dissenting sects, like the Quakers, and had strong Calvinistic beliefs and values.[22]

The Industrial Revolution is often portrayed as man using technology to gain control of the natural world. Here was man using his ingenuity to tame nature and put it to good use. There were thought to be few limits to what nature could provide, if only we could develop the right sorts of technology to exploit it. This gave rise to the illusion of nature as a limitless storehouse, and related illusion of man's limitless creativity and potential. With it came a 'value-vacuum'[23] in which religion was marginalized as belief in progress and technology drove society onwards.

This "value-vacuum" deepened and spread during the eighteenth and nineteenth centuries with the rise of secularism (the rejection of religion). The trend was continued in the nineteenth century as positivism (the view that knowledge can only come from perception) and materialism (interest in possessions rather than spiritual or ethical values) were embraced almost universally, along with scientific rationality and an abiding faith in technological efficiency.

Even greater change was promoted by the development of the doctrine of utilitarianism by British philosophers Jeremy Bentham (1748–1832, founder) and John Stuart Mill (1806–73, developer). Utilitarianism (belief in "the greatest good for the greatest number"[24]) quickly became the basis for ethics and behaviour. A further catalyst was the debate about the class struggle and the formation of the basis of modern communism by Karl Marx (1818–83), Friedrich Engels (1820–95) and Vladimir Ilyich Lenin (1870–1924).

This was the age of industrialization, and it is no accident that it was also the first age of massive and widespread environmental damage and destruction. The die was cast for further increases in resource-use, pollution and desecration of the environment in the twentieth century. By now the trends were almost unstoppable. The rise during the eighteenth and nineteenth centuries of the secular, rational, science-based world-view had created the basis for today's utilitarian, technological, consumptive society whose single-minded pursuit of material progress would in turn create today's environmental crisis.

Technocracy and scientism

Many of the values and attitudes first identified in the eighteenth and nineteenth centuries have survived through to today. Our modern mechanistic world-view has two hallmarks – an almost unquestioned belief in science (scientism), and a pervasive dependence on technology and efficiency (technocracy).

Modern science has created many of the products

which today we take for granted but which have radically altered the quality of human life. Obvious examples include the non-stick pan (indeed almost all of our cooking appliances, including microwaves, freezers and food-processors), the motor car (again, extending to all forms of modern transport), the computer (and all forms of technology for storing, handling and communicating information), and modern medicines and medical equipment. Our is a science-based existence, of that there's little doubt.

But science does not come free, and it does not come without limitations and problems. There is no shortage of critics of modern science. Many argue that environmental problems arise largely because of the way that science is used in modern society.[25] The problem is not science *per se*, it is what we do with it.

American political scientist Theodore Roszak wrote a book in 1972 called *Where the Wasteland Ends* in which he criticizes three particular short-comings of modern science. The first is reductionism – the view of the world as a machine or a collection of particles in motion, which concentrates on properties like size and speed which can be measured but dismisses properties like beauty and feelings which cannot. The second is objective consciousness. He argues that objectivity (detachment of the observer from what is observed) led to an alienation of man from nature, and the view that nature is an object to be conquered and used. This arrogance towards nature encourages exploitation rather than harmony.

Finally, he criticizes the loss of imagination which science has brought. Science is a routine mechanical process with little place for creative imagination; scientists are interested in the repeatable and general, not the unique. This has encouraged a reduction in the pace and variety of poetic and artistic development, and a more general loss of the sense of awe, wonder and mystery with which people often view the world around them.

Faith in science as a form of knowledge, and *one* way of understanding the world, has removed the shackles of a world-view dependent entirely on cosmology. Critics of science argue that the real problem lies with scientism – the view that science is the *only* form of valid knowledge. Scientism condemns as meaningless all products of the human spirit. It argues that all statements or phenomena which cannot be verified or falsified by empirical testing in the real world have no real meaning. This leaves God out of the picture altogether.

Science and technology go hand-in-hand, and technology brings its own problems. An obvious one is the damage which technology can cause, through environmental degradation or war. Technology concentrates power in the hands of a small group of people – power over nature, and power over other people. Modern society relies on experts who can understand the complexities of technical questions, so that technocrats (technical specialists and highly trained elites)[26] make many of society's most important decisions, such as whether to embark on a national programme of building nuclear power stations. Technology also helps to dehumanize man. In modern Western society, where mass production and mass media, uniformity and standardization are the norm, man is in many ways just a cog in a well-oiled and highly organized machine. He feels and indeed largely is subservient to the machines. As such he is largely powerless to change anything within the vast impersonal bureaucracy of which he is but a small part.

We seem to have an almost unquestioned belief in man's technological omnipotence, believing that we will be able to do anything we like so long as we invest enough in appropriate research and development.[27] Equally, we seem to be imprisoned by the so-called technological imperative, believing that if we have developed a particular type of technology, we *must* use it . . . even if we know it to be a mixed blessing (think of nuclear energy, or nuclear weapons, for example).

So the scientism and technocracy which underlie modern Western societies are powerful influences on attitudes and values. Both are firmly rooted in the mechanistic world-view, and both assume that nature is there to be used and controlled. For many people the ultimate goal of life is to accumulate goods and wealth, success is measured in materialistic terms, individualism (and thus pleasure-seeking and personal fulfilment) is of the essence, and humanism has replaced faith and cosmology.

ECOLOGICAL WORLD-VIEWS

The ecological world-views focus on harmony between man and nature, and represent radical alternatives to the mechanistic world-views. Here we find the basis for today's widespread interest in the environment.

Romanticism

The origins of today's ecology movement lie deep in history, but its immediate roots lie in the Romantic movement of the late eighteenth and nineteenth centuries. The Romantic movement in art, music and literature grew out of opposition to the classical style which had been so popular in eighteenth-century Europe and had been heavily influenced by the formalism in art and culture typical of ancient Greece and Rome.

The main emphasis within Romanticism was on feeling rather than form, on the sublime and exotic rather than the everyday, and on free expression of passion and individuality rather than oppressed conformity.[28] Romantics were soulful idealists, unashamed sentimentalists, interested in adventure and mystery.

Nature had special meaning for the Romantics as a source of mystery and imagination. Far from dominating nature, as the mechanistic world-views would have it, man was dominated by nature. The seasons, the elements, wilderness, landscapes and wildlife were important triggers of human emotions and symbols of some grand unity within the universe of which man is but a minute part.

The revolt against modern science and technology was led by French philosopher and writer Jean Jacques Rousseau (1712–78), who believed that man is naturally good but is usually adversely influenced by society. The real problem, he concluded, is that society deprives the individual of his freedom and humanity by imposing artificial needs on him – the need to conform, to work, to possess things, to have (and demonstrate) status and power, to progress, and so on.

Rousseau's solution was to advocate that we should try to regain our lost humanity, by effectively opting out of society and returning to nature (and thus to ourselves). Walking away from materialism, consumerism, scientism, technocentrism and all the other cultural baggage of modern life was not, to him, a sign of defeat or weakness. Quite the opposite. It is a sign of inner strength and wisdom, of humanity reclaiming its roots and re-establishing itself on a more sustainable basis. In both senses (diagnosis of the problem, and prognosis of the solution) modern green writers can rightly claim Rousseau as one of their most influential forefathers.

Implicit in Rousseau's world-view is a new concept of nature, not as an object for exploration to satisfy our material needs but as part of our inherent spirituality. Nature is an ideal where the individual and the outside world are at one with each other. It is a situation of mutual interest between man and nature.

The first leading figures of the Romantic Movement were the English poets. William Wordsworth (1770–1850) conveyed a deep and affectionate feeling for nature in his writings. His work not only describes nature, it celebrates it. He revolutionized poetry through a number of major works, and is generally regarded as the first example of English romantic poetry. Other leading Romantic writers include Wordsworth's friend, the poet and critic Samuel Taylor Coleridge (1772–1834), John Keats (1795–1821), Lord Byron (1788–1824) and Percy Shelley (1792–1822).

It would be over-stretching the point to assume that their works were read by everyone throughout the land and thus influenced a whole generation's thinking and views. But the popularity of their poems and other writings is a useful barometer of general feelings, and provides a hint of the passion with which many people saw and continue to see the natural world around them.

The Romantics value nature as uplifting and inspirational. In some ways the Romantics see nature as a mirror of all that is good within man (reflecting qualities like harmony, naturalness and stability). They see technology, on the other hand, as a mirror of all that is bad within man (reflecting qualities like corruption, power, exploitation, greed and materialism).

Many people, then and now, can bridge the mechanistic and the ecological world-views through the weekly cycle of work and play.[29] At work the "conqueror of nature" view often prevails, if only because many of us have jobs which reflect the technocratic system which underlies modern society. But at weekends and during vacations, we can enjoy the luxury of a Romantic view through the pleasure of trips to the countryside, fell-walking, climbing and so on.

Darwinism

The Romantic movement represented a nineteenth-century reaction within the arts against mechanism of all forms. But reactions also appeared within science. During the nineteenth century the notion of progressive change and adaptation began to emerge, within the Romantic movement and within the debate about relationships between man and society initiated by Karl Marx.[30]

It was within biology that we see the most rapid and far-reaching rise of evolutionary theory, especially after the publication in 1859 of Charles Darwin's *Origin of Species*. Darwin was not the first to suggest that species can change progressively through time, but he was first to propose the mechanism of natural selection (literally, survival of the fittest) as the primary means of evolutionary change. In his view, organisms are naturally adapted to their environments by natural selection. Over many successive generations the individuals within a given species which survive and reproduce best will tend to be those best suited to their environment.

Thus by arguing and indeed demonstrating that all species are interrelated and are intimately related to environment, Darwin effectively restored the idea of wholeness and interrelationships in nature. The Darwinian world-view is that man and nature are inherently inter-related. Man does not fully control nature, and nature does not fully control man; both control each other.

The progressive acceptance of Darwin's views on evolution encouraged the rise of scientific ecology. Ecology, derived from the Greek word *oikos* (meaning house, or environment), is the study of the relationships between living organisms and their environment. From a background in natural history and inspired by the writings of literary naturalists (such as Richard Jefferies in Britain, and John Muir and John Burroughs in the United States), the first generation of ecologists established the subject on a scientific basis.

Critics of the reductionism of modern science welcome the holism of modern ecology, which focuses on unity and interrelationships.[31] One particularly prominent early ecologist was Aldo Leopold, whose widely-read 1949 book *Sand County Almanac* includes a powerful call for a "land ethic" and an "ecological conscience". Leopold concluded that conservation will not be serious business until it has become a concern for philosophy and theology. In this way he foresaw the emergence of a broader public interest in ecology, through today's ecology movement. For the same reason he has been revered by many modern green writers as a visionary and luminary.

Shallow and deep ecology

The ecology movement spans many different viewpoints and sets of values, because people are committed to the ecological world-view for different reasons, in different ways, and to different extents. Many writers try to pigeon-hole people into two groups, which in reality represent the end-points of a continuous spectrum of viewpoints.

The so-called "shallow ecology" group is fundamentally man-centred (anthropocentric), arguing that nature should be protected because it is valuable to people in different ways. Shallow ecologists[32] believe that although modern science, technology and politics have played significant roles in creating environmental problems, each can be altered for the better. Their preferred way forward, therefore, given that we have a serious environmental crisis, involves better design and new technologies (such as using wood not plastics, or wool not synthetic yarns), and reformed politics (socialist governments).

At the other end of the spectrum, the so-called "deep ecology" group is fundamentally nature-centred (ecocentric), arguing that nature is valuable in its own right, irrespective of whether it has utility to man. Deep ecologists[33] prefer mysticism to reductionist science, and call for new nature-centred values and a wholesale transformation of society. Arne Naess, who founded Deep Ecology, argues that it does not have a discrete philosophy and is not a rigid dogma, but rather "a platform that draws together supporters from disparate backgrounds and gives them a base from which to reassess humanity's relationship with Nature".[34]

This platform has a number of central beliefs. Deep ecologists recognize that all life-forms are inherently valuable and they are concerned for the richness and diversity of life on earth. They argue that people have no right to reduce this richness and diversity except to satisfy vital needs. They call for a substantial decrease in the number of people on earth and a reduction of the amount of human interference with nature. This requires radical changes in the policies which affect the basic economic, technological and ideological structures of modern society, along with a re-ordering of priorities towards quality of life and away from material standards of living.

Postmodernism

We are starting to see signs of the emergence of what sociologists call a "postmodern, postmaterialist" world-view[35] which is fundamentally ecological in emphasizing harmony between man and nature. It appears in much contemporary green writing which stresses the merits of environmental lifestyles and products. Qualities such as craftsmanship, distinctiveness, functionality, design and durability are starting to be taken seriously, not simply out of fashion but because they produce less waste and use fewer material resources.

Taken to the extreme, this sort of world-view is built upon asceticism (self-denial and abstinence from worldly comforts) and simplicity (the love of simple things and rejection of materialism). The postmodern lifestyle might include leaving a highly-paid city job, selling up and moving to a quiet rural setting, perhaps to farm in a self-sufficient ecological way, or perhaps to start a small-scale craft-business (like painting, making pottery or candles). Whilst such a life doubtless demands great sacrifice in material terms, it brings its own rewards which are treasured more highly than the material hardships – simplicity, closeness to nature, time to think, self-dependence, and modest but sufficient material means.

Postmaterial values are being adopted, perhaps not widely yet. But as more and more people start to find conspicuous consumption offensive as well as wasteful, and realize that worth or value might be better measured in terms of creativity or decency, not just price or size, the world-view spreads. If such views persist and are more widely adopted, nature stands to gain a great deal.

Nature, to the postmodernist, is a source of pleasure and creative inspiration as well as a source of raw materials. The ascetic lifestyles favoured by some modern writers, green and non-green, elevate nature to the same status as man.

PART TWO

GREEN SPIRITUALITY

CHAPTER FOUR

Spiritual Warfare

There is no denying the link between spirituality and the environmental crisis, and the crisis turns out to be one of the soul perhaps more than of science and technology. British green David Icke writes about a deep spirit within us, noting how "it is our soul that is moved by beauty, nature, art, words, and emotions . . . our souls have been imprisoned since the start of the industrial revolution . . . our souls have become trapped and tortured inside us, resulting in depression, despair, a lack of fulfilment, and a deep sense that 'there must be more to life than this'."[1]

The green debate is partly about whether material and spiritual issues can be fully reconciled, and whether the world can continue to support the gross materialism of modern society.

Whether or not spirituality is synonymous with dedication to God or "being religious" depends largely on the belief systems of the individual. For example the Christian accepts God as creator and sustainer of all things in the universe, whereas eastern religions and philosophies tend to find ultimate meanings more within the individual person.

Spirituality, which acknowledges that there is something beyond the material world that we can experience directly, is concerned with ultimate meanings or purposes. It shares much with cosmology (the philosophical study of the origin and nature of the universe) and metaphysics (the study of first principles and assumptions), and it reflects fundamental beliefs about reality and meaning (world-views). In the particular context of the green debate, spirituality is based on trying to understand our relationship with the earth.

Spiritual search

Many people have commented upon the apparently widespread search for real values and ultimate meanings in society today. As we approach the end of the century – indeed, the end of the millennium – what sociologists refer to as postmodern, postliberal, postsocialist or postconservative society turns out to be seriously devoid of spiritual values. Our widespread spiritual hunger reflects a genuine desire amongst many people to better understand how they fit into the great order of things. It also seems to reflect a broader interest in human fulfilment, involving spiritual, intellectual, artistic and cultural growth ... rather than simply the accumulation of material products or the pursuit of power.

Christians are by no means the only group to recognize the spiritual nature of the environmental crisis.[2] People's concern for the environment is an inherently spiritual matter. Indeed, it might be that interest in green issues offers a contemporary vehicle for mobilizing wide public interest in spiritual matters. But to the Christian this is a double-edged sword. The good news is the opportunities which might be presented to share the Gospel of Christ and the Christian message of love, forgiveness and a new beginning. The bad news is the problems which arise in identifying and competing against the spectrum of philosophical and spiritual groups who are exploiting people's concern for the environment.

It is very much a spiritual battleground, in which the

battle for people's souls is being fought on the ground of environmental concern. Many of the skirmishes go unnoticed, yet there may be many spiritual casualties as individuals are unsuspectingly seduced into unhealthy spiritual practices and beliefs via their search for kindred spirits in the environmental movement.

Spiritual roots of environmental concern

This modern spiritual battle centred on interest in environment has roots which go back to the wave of environmental activism and social rebellion which swept across the USA in the 1960s.[3] It was a remarkable period of rapid cultural change, with fierce opposition to racial discrimination, widespread condemnation of the Vietnam war, and student unrest in the USA and in Paris. It witnessed the emergence of the new hippy counterculture, shaped under the liberating influence of psychedelic drugs (like LSD) and new youth-centred music (from the likes of Bob Dylan, Joni Mitchell and the Beatles).

Many hippies and sympathizers looked towards the religions and philosophies of the east for a new set of values and lifestyles compatible with ecology and conservation. Zen Buddhism and Taoism in particular were widely embraced, as the late 60s hippy environmentalists sought new spiritual awareness and liberation from "the system".[4]

Out of this wave of concern for environment and its underlying current of social turmoil and counterculture activism, has evolved one of the major strands of spirituality within today's green movement. It represents a strange mixture of ingredients from different backgrounds which have coalesced into the "deep ecology" movement which emphasizes unity and harmony, and takes its main practical cues from ecology and its spiritual cues from New Age thinking and mysticism.

Christianity under attack

Interest in environment and interest in spirituality have grown in parallel over the past three decades. But not only has the Christian Church largely ignored the unfolding green debate, it has been strongly attacked in it.

One particular camp within the green movement is highly critical of Christianity. Its champion was US historian of science Lynn White, who published a paper in the journal *Science* in 1967 called "The historical roots of our ecological crisis". In it he laid the blame for the environmental crisis squarely on Christianity, arguing that the Christian teaching of domination over creation (particularly the commands in Genesis to "subdue" the earth and have "dominion" over all creatures) has encouraged exploitative and damaging attitudes and behaviour, which are the ultimate causes of the environmental crisis. Many green writers have since repeated the charge.[5]

Tensions exist between green activists and the Christian Church because of these sorts of attitudes and accusations which are both unhealthy and unfounded. Indeed, the tensions seem to be getting deeper and stronger through time, as more and more green writers echo White's arguments and seek simple solutions in two main ways. One popular approach is to endorse un-Christian or anti-Christian philosophies and ideologies (like the New Age movement). The second solution is to advocate that the environment becomes the focus of a new popular religion in its own right.

TRADITIONAL BELIEF SYSTEMS

A recurrent theme in much green writing is the inferred aridity and emptiness of modern religions compared with traditional religions. Traditional belief-systems, it is argued, were based on respect for nature and on a view of life which emphasized continuity with spirits of ancestors and with sacred sites.

Native peoples, pagan beliefs and sacred sites

Such a perspective finds two outlets – a growing interest in pagan beliefs, and a growing interest in the belief systems of native groups like the North American Indians and African tribes. Paganism (from the Latin *pagani*, meaning country people) emphasizes the sacredness of the earth and its natural cycles and rhythms. Nature mysticism, reverence of Mother Earth, a desire to live in harmony with all of creation, the New Age idea of rebirthing . . . are all offshoots of pagan beliefs.

Many greens assume that native groups like the American Indians, the Australian Aborigines and the people of the rainforests had stronger spiritual and emotional ties with their environment than modern society has, so had a better and more instinctive understanding of how to protect it.[6] One reflection of this is the tendency of many native peoples to have sacred sites which they treat with special respect, and which they believe connect them with the planet and may contain special spirits linked with their ancestors or with special gods. The Aborigines, who from time to time recharge their spiritual batteries by going walkabout amongst sacred ancestral sites, provide a graphic example.

African traditional religion is also heavily orientated towards respect for nature and living in harmony with it.[7] It is based on belief in one God, who creates and gives all things but has not given people dominion over nature. God's love or anger is seen through natural signs, such as the sun, moon, stars, rain, rainbow, lightning and thunder. There are no temples or churches as such; large trees are worshipped and sacrificed to God. Yet nature worship is not formally part of the religion, which draws no distinction between the spiritual and material worlds. Religion is interwoven with the traditions and social customs of the people. There are no official priests or religious preaching, and Africans believe that they should only approach God indirectly via intermediaries – the seers, prophets, diviners, medicine men, witches, rainmakers, kings, elders, chiefs, ancestors and spirits.

North American Indians

The North American Indians also had special ties to sacred places and to the earth in general.[8] They believed that since human beings have a physical body and a consciousness or spirit, so must all other bodily things (including plants, animals and even stones). Hence, they argued, all things are 'possessed of spirit'. All materials are alive and can help or harm us. We may speak with them, honour or insult them. They are all related together as members of one universal family, born of a father (the sky or Great Spirit) and a mother (the Earth Mother).

The American Indians knew a lot about their natural surroundings, and about which plants and animals they could use for food and medicine. They were conservators who lived in an ecologically-sustainable way.[9] They knew when it was safest to burn trees, for example, without running the risk of firing a whole forest. They grew beans and corn together, to maintain soil fertility. They created hunting preserves for beavers and other animals, to prevent overkill. But it is quite striking that their attitudes and values were driven more by good manners than science. Animals, plants, and minerals were treated as persons and seen as having similar status.[10]

Spiritual unity amongst all creation underlies the much-quoted 1885 speech of Indian Chief Seattle, in which he said, "The earth does not belong to man, man belongs to the earth. This we know. All things are connected. Whatever befalls the earth befalls the sons of the earth. Man did not weave the web of life, he is merely a strand in it. Whatever he does to the web, he does to himself . . .".[11]

LOOKING EAST

Some people engaged in a personal search for a proper spiritual basis for environmentalism have looked towards the various belief systems of the orient. These contrast markedly with traditional Western religions, through their tendency to demand an empathy with nature, their emphasis on self-discovery and self-realization within the individual person, and their down-playing of the pursuit of wealth and power. They apparently had much to offer the spiritually confused – or, by self-proclamation, spiritually liberated – 1960s dedicated followers of fashion.

Taoism

One particular brand of oriental belief system which – its followers claimed – offered the foundation for a sounder ecological lifestyle, was the ancient Chinese philosophy of Taoism. Rooted in an emphasis on the need to follow

"The Way" (in essence, to "follow nature"), this had obvious appeal for ecologically-conscious western intellectuals seeking a congenial philosophy.[12]

According to Taoist cosmology, the universe arises out of nothing and will ultimately fall back into nothing. It, and everything in it, is in a constant state of change or transformation – becoming and decaying. Tao is natural order, not a concrete thing; it is the source of everything, and it regulates nature and behaviour. To follow "The Way" is to be in tune with Tao (in line with the natural order of things), and each person has their own programme or Way (tao) which is an integral part of the greater Way (Tao) directed by some invisible hand or power (*not* God) which controls the whole universe.

When things are working properly, the individual taos co-operate and integrate with Tao . . . so it is imperative that each individual finds and lives according to their own tao. Key elements of living well according to Taoism include deep love (involving compassion, care and respect), frugality (in which needs are met adequately without deprivation or excess), and modesty or humility (there is no need for competition).

Followers of Taoism argue that it both requires and creates a high level of ecological consciousness and so it provides a practical basis for a way of life based on following nature. Taoism commends a simple, environmentally-sound life style based on love, respect and compassion for all things, using only what is essential and shedding what is not.[13] It is a life style based on simplicity and frugality. Nature is seen as something to be cherished and allowed to take its own course, not interfered with or destroyed. Here, some greens argue, is the basis for a sustainable good life which rejects Western obsession with wealth, possessions, power, prestige and competition.

Zen Buddhism

A similar emphasis on unity and interdependence figures prominently in Zen Buddhism, which many greens claim is the most nature-oriented religion and has many parallels with ecology.[14] They argue that the root of the environmental crisis can be traced in the dualism of Western thought which promotes antagonistic attitudes towards nature and encourages people to exploit nature as something external to themselves. Western man is an activist, driven by the motto "when in doubt, do something".

Zen, in contrast, favours inaction and a pattern of behaviour which preserves nature. It sees the world as an organic whole, in which all things are fundamentally interconnected. For the individual, the challenge of Zen is to achieve pure enlightenment, which is approached by contemplating one's essential nature to the exclusion of all else. In Buddhist belief, enlightenment is a state of spiritual revelation which brings an awakening to ultimate truth, by which a person is freed from the endless cycle of reincarnations to which all people are otherwise naturally and eternally subjected.

An intimate relationship with nature lies at the very heart of Buddhist belief.[15] The world and its people have evolved together over a vast period of time, man and nature are governed by the same universal laws, and changes in the environment cause changes in people. The bond is close and two-way; environmental change is linked with moral change (particularly human lust for power and pleasure). It is Buddhist belief that each person enters into a private relationship with nature via their senses (we see, hear, smell, taste, touch and conceptualize nature), and that our self-centred nature makes us believe that the sense faculties are our own. Consequently suffering in the world could be stopped if sense perception stopped, and the only way to bring this about is by not taking delight in the feelings created by our senses.[16] Thus Buddhism denounces individualism and individual selfishness as evil, and sees man's goal as living in harmony with the moral law that governs the Universe (*dharma*, or destiny).

Buddhism offers a political philosophy based on *dharma* rather than the pursuit of happiness. It has five key ingredients which are interrelated and mutually reinforcing.[17] The first is respectful tolerance, meaning that we should live and let live. Next is equality (both secular and spiritual), requiring that each person should follow their own special vocation (or *dharma*). Third, service, which brings self-purification through loving duty to one's community. Service performed, not results achieved, is all-important. Simplicity is crucial too. It is Buddhist belief that the primary cause of suffering is desire, which makes people constantly want and crave things rather than simply enjoying what they already have. These all support the fifth ingredient, non-violence, not just towards other humans but towards all of creation.

British radical political economist E F Schumacher, a Catholic with great sympathies for Buddhism, wrote in his best selling book *Small is Beautiful* that the goal of economic life should be "Right Livelihood".[18] When this is achieved the economy provides everyone with sufficient material well-being to meet their needs (if not their greed). But the nature of what people do and how they do it are crucial, because their "right livelihoods" are inherently satisfying, do not harm others (either materially or spiritually) and involve the individual in service to his community.[19]

Such an economic order would be characterized by ecological harmlessness and stewardship, a refined simplicity of ends and means alike, and above all a scrupulous regard for the quality of individual human lives. This contrasts sharply with the greed, selfishness, materialism, power, pleasure and control of others which Buddhists argue are promoted by the present economic order.

Buddhism claims to offer both a blueprint for a green lifestyle and the promise of personal enlightenment. Little wonder it was seen as an important and innovative way forward to the spiritual nomads of the 1970s and early 1980s.

Hinduism

Similar themes of self-fulfilment, harmony with the universe and with other people figure prominently within Hinduism, although the green movement has not embraced Hinduism as readily as it has Taoism and Buddhism.

Some Hindus claim that their most ancient books, the Vedas, are really books of ecology which stress that people are part not master of nature.[20] Hindu teaching has it that every part of the universe is a manifestation of God, who has created all things out of spirit (*atman*) and matter (*prakriti*) and placed itself (God) in the centre of all. Thus God is present in every natural thing, and everything is holy for a Hindu. There are holy rivers, holy mountains, holy trees, holy cows, holy men and holy women.

Hindus believe that they are born into *dharma* (the perfect way of living), the objective of which is to find

fulfilment. But fulfilment is defined in terms of equilibrium, not personal satisfaction. There are three ways of
finding this fulfilment – by living in harmony with the
universe (*yajna*), by sharing everything equally among
the members of a community (*dana*), and by living life
in a simply and healthy way such as by fasting, yoga,
meditation, and eating right food (*tapas*). The three are
not mutually exclusive – through *yajna* it is believed
we maintain equilibrium with nature, through *dana* we
maintain equilibrium in society and through *tapas* we
maintain equilibrium within our body. Action without
spiritual consciousness (*mantra*) is regarded as meaningless, whereas with it an action becomes pure and it will
be honouring to God.

Again this form of oriental spirituality suggests the
basis of a proper lifestyle which is environmentally-
sound and hence sustainable.

A New Green Religion?

Green writers have often commented on how ecological-
ly-friendly the oriental belief systems tend to be, and a
brand of green spirituality is starting to emerge which
borrows language, values and sentiments from these
religions (and others) without necessarily embracing all
their practices and customs. This syncretist approach is
founded on the assumption that "all roads lead to Rome",
and that by piecing together an all-embracing and multi-
purpose "religion-for-today" from ingredients drawn
from different cultures, societies and eras it will be possible to arrive at some universal spiritual framework
which transcends time and place and embodies all that
is good and enshrines all that is truthful.

It is perhaps one of the most worrying symptoms of today's green spiritual search, because it capitalizes on a widespread interest in environment and captures people at their most vulnerable. There must be many confused Christians around who have been seduced by the emerging green spirituality and find it hard to determine which bits are compatible with their Christian faith and which bits are not. Similarly, there must be many non-Christian greens who have been seduced into adopting spirituality-speak or into joining fringe groups (or even cults), with the misguided belief that they have discovered the root cause of the environmental crisis and accordingly discovered its solution.

Perhaps just as problematic is the danger of the environment becoming the focus of a new popular religion in its own right. An editorial in *The Times*, on the Monday after the Archbishop of Canterbury preached in Canterbury Cathedral on Christianity and Environment (18 September 1989), pointed out that Christians should be worried about "the threat to Christianity of greenness itself, as it takes on more and more of the characteristics of a religious faith". It continued: "There is already a distinctly mystical fringe to the Green movement."

Just over a week later there was an interesting letter to *The Independent* (28 September 1989), titled Green Goddess? It went as follows:

Dear Sir,
Is green fervour filling the void being left by the demise of popular religion? The resemblances are countless; visionary beliefs, a distaste for material values, a commitment to the life hereafter (future generations), and a saintly tendency to turn the other cheek (weaponless defence). The Green faith-

ful dream of a purer way of life, proclaim the virtues of self denial, tend to prefer emotional zeal to logical analysis and have a kindly but resolute determination to coerce everyone else into adopting their standards of ethical behaviour.

This is a rather odd view of "popular religion", whatever that might be in practice, but it raises a fundamental question. Is the Church missing an important wave of popular concern and morality, or is it deliberately ignoring the passing bandwagon? The answer appears to be "both", to some extent.

Nature worship

One of the dangers in the green field today is the prospect of being drawn into pantheism, worship of the natural world. This can be much more subtle and seductive than we might imagine, and it is often very difficult to know where to draw the line between appreciating nature and worshipping it. We must be careful to avoid focusing reverence on nature, and direct it instead to what nature can reveal about its creator. Taken to extreme, pantheism draws us into paganism – a semi-religious faith based on sacredness of the earth and its cycles and seasons. Many of today's green writers are putting forward a brand of spirituality which is little short of pagan.

Nature worship is doubtless on the increase, and in some ways it reflects a backlash against the clinical excesses of modern scientism. Whatever the motive, this trend is a worrying one for Christians, who see nature as a sign of God's creation, care and everyday involvement in the world. Nature is a window to God; it is *not*, in itself, God. As the editorial in *The Times*[21] put it, "The worship of nature ... and the worship of the one God who created nature, are two very different and essentially incompatible religions".

The most "green" event in the Christian calendar is the Harvest Festival. This is a celebration of God's bounty and a thanksgiving for God's grace and love . . . it is not a worship of the Harvest produce *per se*!

Gaia

Without doubt the most popular green way of looking at the earth and everything on it today is in terms of Gaia, a theory proposed in the early 1970s by scientist-inventor James Lovelock who named it after the ancient earth goddess of the Greeks.[22] It is based on the idea that the planet is alive, and functions as a kind of superorganism in which living things interact with the planet's environment to maintain conditions suitable for life. It borrows heavily from the classical Greek world-view.

According to the Gaia hypothesis[23] the earth's atmosphere would be unstable for life if it were not regulated by the earth's plants and animals and by its environmental systems. Lovelock's original idea was that Gaia followed some purposeful design which organized living things to stabilize the atmosphere and climate. The notion that the earth acted with some sense of purpose in seeking to achieve a predefined goal received widespread criticism and Lovelock has since refined the idea to allow for regulation through the mechanism of feedback (via internal interrelationships).

Gaia is a self-regulating system. The system is highly organized and hierarchical, and all of its components play a part in creating and maintaining stability, which is the ultimate goal. If one part of the system changes, or is changed, the rest of the system will adapt so as to maintain stability.

If the Gaian system is goal-directed, as Lovelock proposed, then it suggests some form of pre-programming with relevant instructions; the instructions are endowed, and are provided sequentially as and when required. This inevitably raises the thorny question "Who did the programming and why?".[24] The Christian quickly replies that surely this is evidence of God's handiwork and continued interest in his creation. Supporters of Gaia have no answer, other than the vague notion of the invisible hand of some universal force (certainly not God) holding it all together and making it all work.[25]

Although the hypothesis was first suggested in the early 1970s, it is only recently that scientists have started to take it seriously. But its terminology and basic ideas are being assimilated fast into the green movement, who welcome it as a useful vehicle for tying together material and non-material properties of life on earth. Gaian ideas have been warmly embraced by New Age thinkers, who particularly like its holistic view of nature. This has opened up Lovelock's ideas to a much wider audience than the scientists who initially debated the hypothesis, and it has added a veneer of unorthodox spirituality to the already troubled waters of Gaian science.

The New Age movement

There is no doubt that the green debate has been strongly shaped by so-called New Age thinkers and practitioners.

The movement has roots in the freedom movement and in astrology and the occult. Its central belief is that, in astrological terms, the world is about to leave the Age of Pisces (which corresponds roughly with the Christian era) and enter a new utopian Age of Aquarius (which is to dawn some time between now and 2062). Hence "New Age". Founded on the atheistic presupposition that everything is explainable without a need to invoke a supernatural God, its ultimate objective is syncretist – the unity of all religions. Christian theologian and writer John Stott describes the New Age movement as "an uneasy blend of eastern mysticism and western materialism, of science and superstition, of Yin and Yang (the feminine and the masculine), of space and time, of physics and metaphysics, of ancient wisdom and new consciousness".[26]

New Agers deny the existence of good and evil in the world and in people, and they see authority as internal; it comes from within the individual (the god or Force within) rather than from an external God. So they believe they are already divine and have endless potential for self-improvement. The New Age movement is strong on human potential, believing that every person is god and needs only to have their consciousness enlightened to realize this. According to New Age thinking the basic human predicament is not moral (sin and guilt) but metaphysical (ignorance of our own true identity). To them salvation is found within through self-realization made possible by a consciousness altered not by drugs but via techniques such as yoga, visualization and crystals.

There is also a strong belief in reincarnation and cyclical forms of life, borrowed from oriental religions. Spiritism and channeling are also key New Age beliefs and practices; "channels" are individuals who believe their bodies are taken over by spirits from another dimension. New Agers are often associated with witchcraft and other occult practices.

It is a pervasive movement with a lucrative and visible commercial spearhead. Many mainstream magazines regularly carry advertisements for products such as relaxation or self-awareness tapes, exotic crystals and paraphernalia of the occult. Perhaps understandably, few carry the label New Age, and it is often difficult to detect the true origins or intentions of such merchandising. Some clues are offered by the symbols favoured by New Agers, which often appear on their products – especially rainbows, pyramids, triangles, eyes in triangles, unicorns and yin-yan, (two black and white comma shapes joined together in a circle).[27] This is a particularly subtle but dangerous form of spiritual infiltration, especially the use of rainbow signs, which unsuspecting purchasers will often assume to be either innocent or Christian.

The New Age movement has grown rapidly in recent decades, capitalizing on the spiritual vacuum in many people's lives and on the growing interest in direct spiritual experiences and in the paranormal (science fiction, fantasy, role-play, the occult). Other factors which have conspired to promote the spread of the movement include a growing concern for world peace and global political co-operation, growing dissatisfaction with orthodox medicine, and development of the New Physics and Biology.[28]

One estimate is that there are up to 60 million people aligned with the New Age movement in the USA alone,[29] but precise figures are impossible to come by because the movement is such a loose coalition of groups and individuals working round the world for global unity, peace and harmony with nature.

The New Age movement and the green movement converge in a number of ways, which at times blur the edges between them and create a coalition which has widespread popular appeal but raises profound spiritual problems. Both movements, for example, promote vegetarian diets and holistic (alternative) medicine, and both crusade for animal rights and ecology.

Both are underpinned by a fundamental concern for

conservation and protection of unity in the cosmos, and this opens many people to earth mysticism and pantheism. The Archbishop of Canterbury was issued with dire warnings in the summer of 1989 about the New Age influence upon those concerned with green issues, especially surrounding the Festival of Faith and the Environment organized by the World-Wide Fund for Nature (WWF) at Canterbury in September 1989. He later wrote of the New Age movement that "it tends to find its main expression politically in the green movement and personally in spiritual ideas often, but not exclusively, associated with astrology. Yet many members and supporters of the Green Party would not be New Agers, and not all New Agers are into ecology or astrology". He also conceded that the problem with the movement is that "it is so boundaryless that Christians are sometimes left with an uncomfortable feeling about their participation in ecological events or creation liturgies, not so much about what they actually say or do not say, but what they might be implicitly endorsing without knowing it".[30]

John Stott dismisses the New Age movement as "a counterfeit and a fraud" which is incompatible with Christianity.[31] Yet by its subtle infiltration into people's lives (for example through merchandising of "ecological" products), by the widespread spiritual search which many people are engaged in today (often without realizing it as such), and by its strong attachment to the green movement, the New Age movement poses one of the greatest threats to the development of an acceptable green spirituality today.

A NICHE FOR CHRISTIANS?

It is clear that most world faiths have something to say about nature and the environment, and many of them have won supporters and even converts from within the green movement. What is also clear is that Christianity has been more of a loser than a winner in this spiritual battle – heavily criticized as a root cause of the environmental crisis and more a focus of attack than defence.

So, where are the Christians in this debate? Their voice has not been loud, and their presence not too obvious – despite a long tradition of Christian interest and involvement in caring for the environment and managing it wisely.

The lack of overt Christian interest in the environmental debate seems to stem from four main factors which have been prominent within twentieth-century theology. One is a natural preoccupation with people and personal salvation, which emphasizes human nature rather than nature. Thus the material world is viewed as a backdrop or stage for the drama of human existence; the actor substantially more relevant and important than the scenery. Whilst there are passages in the Gospels which reinforce this view (such as Romans 12:2 which instructs us to conform no longer to the pattern of the world), they must be set into the broader context of appreciating that God created and cares for the whole universe.

The second factor is an underlying lack of deep concern amongst many Christians for the long-term future of planet earth. It may rarely appear in such stark definition, but it is a defensible position given the Christian's belief in a "new heaven and a new earth" which Christ will create when he returns, the old ones having passed away (see, for example, 2 Peter 3:13 and Revelation 21:4). A rather extreme view is thus that the sooner this new earth arrives the better, because it will herald the return to earth of Jesus. Why, therefore, should we prolong the present earth or intervene in its decay which is ordained by God (as Psalm 102 and others insist) anyway?

Of course such a position makes an implicit assumption that this earth is expendable, which is clearly not the case. It is God's creation and we are supposed to be looking after it until his son Jesus Christ returns. God alone will decide on the timing of that return, and in the meantime we must accept our responsibilities as God's guardians of his created earth and its natural wealth and beauty.

Thirdly, there is the argument that the environmental debate is a political battleground, and Christianity and politics simply don't mix. But this position is unfounded because Christianity is rooted in the battle between right and wrong, good and bad.

Finally, many Christians point to the obvious dangers of an unhealthy preoccupation with the material world, which brings with it the danger of worshiping false gods (like Mother Earth, or animal spirits) or condoning unacceptable spiritual practices (like the occult, or animal sacrifices to appease "the gods"). To focus on the created world rather than on the creator would be to undervalue the sovereignty of God. It is fine and indeed inspiring to marvel at the world as God's handiwork, but we need to see through that (rather like looking through a window) to God's perfection, care, love and interest in every part of his creation.

The green movement is a spiritual battleground. Many greens have a strong empathy with traditional religions and oriental belief-systems, and values and practices from both have been borrowed in the fabrication of a new green spirituality. But this shift in the axis of spirituality, away from a concern for the soul of people and towards a concern for the soul of the planet, is viewed with deep concern by many Christians. Naturally it raises the question "Why has it happened?", or – perhaps more correctly – "Why has it been allowed to happen?".

There are two possible answers. One is that Christianity has failed to claim and hold on to the spiritual (or moral) high ground and make its claim heard and felt. The ground may have been given away from inside. The second possibility is that new (and arguably false) philosophies have spotted the opportunity to seize this ground and build a strong base of popular support on it. The ground may have been high-jacked from outside.

Doubtless both explanations are partly true. But this emerging green spirituality is an important signal that many people's spiritual needs are not being met and it shows that people must have a cause to believe in. Whether it turns out to be a threat to Christian values and principles will depend mainly on whether the spiritual high ground is reclaimed by Christians. After all, the popular interest in green issues might create all sorts of opportunities to set the record straight about the role of Christianity in causing the environmental crisis, and in turn open doors for more positive sharing of the Gospel.

In terms of green issues, therefore, Christianity appears to be at an important crossroads with two ways forward. One is to jump on the green bandwagon and try to turn it round to its proper (biblical) direction. The alternative is to sit back and watch it pass by, hoping that it does so quickly, without attracting too many innocent people on board.

CHAPTER FIVE

CHRISTIANITY IN THE DOCK

The green movement represents a major challenge for Christianity, which is threatened in two ways. One is the indirect attack from the other main world faiths which the green movement endorses, to which many greens are in danger of drifting if they think that Christianity offers nothing relevant to their interests and needs. There is also the direct attack from those who accuse Christianity of having caused and subsequently perpetuated values, attitudes and behaviour which lead directly to serious environmental damage.

This direct attack started in the late 60s and was championed by Lynn White, a medieval historian from the University of California, Los Angeles.

THE WHITE THESIS

White published a paper in the international journal *Science* in 1967, entitled "The historical roots of our ecological crisis". It quickly became a landmark within the environmental debate.

His central argument is that the ruthless treatment of nature by Western science and technology which now threatens all life on earth has roots in the exploitive attitude toward nature which was created and sustained by Judaism and Christianity. He declared that because of "orthodox Christian arrogance toward nature", Christianity "bears a huge burden of guilt" for the contemporary ecological crisis.[1]

The argument

White points out that the first major environmental problems began to emerge (at least in Europe) at the end of the medieval period, for two reasons – both related to Christianity. First, developments in technology at this time were allowing people more control over their environment. Secondly, the Christian concept of man's relation to nature (the view that all of nature was created by God for mankind's benefit) was being more widely accepted.

White's thesis is built on the premise that beliefs shape behaviour; what people do about their environment (how they view it and use it) reflects what they think about themselves in relation to things about them. So the central thread is that beliefs about nature and destiny condition how we use the environment.

He then singles out Christianity as the most people-centred (anthropocentric) of the major world religions, pointing out that non-Western religions tend not to separate man from nature. Western Christianity established a dualism between man and nature, he argues, because no item in the physical creation had any purpose other than to serve man.

White argues that Genesis 1:26–8 gives a mandate for tyrannical human control over nature. Those verses describe how, after creating the universe, living creatures and then people, "God blessed them, and said to them, 'Be fruitful and increase in number; fill the earth and subdue it. Rule over the fish of the sea and the birds of the air and over every living creature that moves on the ground'." This gave believers in Christianity a licence to damage the environment, so "the Judeo-Christian tradition is responsible for the desecration of nature in the Western world".[2] He goes so far as to insist that the Bible says "it is God's will that man exploit nature for his proper ends".[3]

As Christianity spread, older pagan beliefs in the sacredness of places and natural things (which tended to unite man and nature) were destroyed. This encouraged more people to damage and exploit the environment with total indifference to any rights of wildlife and natural objects.

Another thread in the thesis is the link between biblical views on creation, and the development of science and technology. Man was created to be master over the rest of creation; he was, after all, created after the plants, animals and fishes. This naturally encouraged the development of Western science, technology and industrialization which lie at the root of the environmental crisis.

White argued that modern technology grew within Western (Latin) Christianity – the Roman Catholic and later the Protestant Churches – not within the Eastern tradition (Islam or Eastern Orthodoxy) because the Latin style is active while the Greek Church is contemplative. Hence man's impact on nature is most severe in the West, he concluded. Christianity also gave rise to Western man's implicit faith in perpetual progress (an idea unknown to ancient Greece and Rome and to the Orient), which further encouraged the development and adoption of technology.

White also ties in changing attitudes towards nature and the religious motives on which they were built. He argues that before about 1400 nature was studied as a way of finding out more about God. After 1400 Western scientists started to study physical processes of light and matter, but it was still done in the name of religious progress. So Christianity had a strong influence on the development of Western science, at least between the thirteenth and the eighteenth centuries.

The conclusion

After piecing together the jigsaw of his argument, White cannot avoid drawing the conclusion that "both our present science and our present technology are so tinctured with orthodox Christian arrogance toward nature that no solution for our ecological crisis can be expected from them alone. Since the roots of our trouble are so largely religious, the remedy must also be essentially religious, whether we call it that or not ... We must rethink and refeel our nature and destiny".[4]

His was a "no holds barred" attack on the teachings of Christianity. He insisted, for example, that "we shall continue to have a worsening ecological crisis until we reject the Christian axiom that nature has no reason for existence save to serve man". Yet he surprised many people by suggesting that the solution may lie within rather than outside Christianity. Interestingly, this fact is often overlooked by those who have since repeated White's thesis to support their claim that ecologists' interests are better served by other religions, particularly Oriental ones.

White's solution is a return to the humble attitudes of the early Franciscans. The paper concludes with a proposal that St Francis of Assisi be adopted as the patron saint for ecologists. Francis treated all of nature's creatures as if they possessed souls to be saved (like man), not as if they were there simply to be used. As White sees it, Francis tried to depose man from his monarchy over creation and set up a democracy of all God's creatures. This alternative, non-exploitive attitude is necessary, he thinks, rather than one of domination and exploitation.

The reaction

Many writers have commented on White's paper, its message and its impact. But White was not the first to develop this particular line of argument, and "Historical roots" has historical roots of its own. Its major premise, that the Western Christian tradition is indirectly responsible for the rise of science and technology (which made it possible for man to conquer and dominate nature), has been debated for a good many years.[5]

Yet it was the paper in *Science* which achieved immediate fame. It was widely reprinted and quoted. Its thesis was often borrowed (with and without acknowledgement), as if it were established fact. White himself was apparently very surprised by the reaction.[6] The question "Why did this particular paper have such instant appeal, and such an amazing reception around the world?" is rarely asked, but it is important to think about.

Several factors conspired to make the paper so popular. It was well written, by "an engaging raconteur with a gift for the memorable phrase and the arresting thought".[7] It appeared in a journal with a wide circulation and was instantly accessible to scientists around the world, so it had a vast number of potential readers. It was also about a topic which the scientific community rarely thinks about – religion and ecology. It had the right tone, too, and was widely viewed as provocative. It wasn't a soft-sell for religion; quite the opposite. It also appeared at the right time, particularly to be adopted by the counter-culture groups which were appearing in the early 1970s and exploring new forms of spirituality (especially Oriental ones).

It had an appeal which went far beyond the boundaries of science, and was often interpreted and used in ways contrary to White's original intent. The irony is that Lynn White, a Christian with a genuine concern for Christianity, was deliberately looking in the paper for new attitudes within Christianity, not outside it. Yet almost without exception those who have enthusiastically seized on his thesis and used it to promote their own particular agendas are anti-Christian types with a mixture of personal motives.[8]

EVALUATION OF THE THESIS

The Lynn White paper has probably had a bigger impact on green thinking than just about any other single piece of writing. It has played an important role in opening up the ecology-religion debate, and inviting the Christian Church to respond to his accusations. Yet Christian response to the paper and its arguments has been very muted. The thesis is open to criticism on several grounds.

1. Does belief control behaviour?

White's central argument is that religious belief directly controls the way people behave, which in turn affects nature and the environment. But is it so simple? Would a change in attitudes automatically bring an end to the environmental crisis?

Evidence from around the world, from different cultures and different times, shows repeatedly that actual habits (such as land-use practices) often depart significantly from what the ethical ideals of that society suggest. This is true even when that society believes that nature or land is sacred. Many studies have shown that even societies with reverential attitudes towards environment have spoiled their environments. The Oriental religions, which on the surface have many positive things to say about harmony with nature, have not always prevented environmental damage. China, for example, has a long history of soil erosion and forest clearance.[9]

A culture's environmental beliefs and environmental impacts might be only loosely associated because there may be inherent inconsistencies within the belief-systems. For example, the early American pioneers had strong beliefs in fundamentalist Christianity (with its inherent aversion to worldly riches), yet they also had a self-centred materialistic view towards nature (it was there for them to use).[10]

Any attempt to portray environmental attitudes in a simple way is difficult, anyway, for several reasons. First, the evidence is often fragmentary and partial. Can we really understand the environmental attitudes of ordinary people in ancient Greece simply by looking at the surviving writings of a few Greek philosophers?[11] Secondly, the evidence is often contradictory – even within one primary source. The Bible is notoriously difficult to interpret unambiguously, and Christian scholars often disagree between themselves over the environmental message of the Bible.[12]

Added difficulty comes from the inevitable fact that each person who shares the beliefs of a particular religion is an individual, not a pre-programmed machine. They see things differently, understand things differently, have different strengths of faith and different tolerance levels for "bending the rules". Some Christians are strict in their efforts to lead a proper Christian life while others are less so, just as some Buddhists are more strict with themselves, and so on. This is not a feature of any particular religion, it is a fact of life.

So the assumption that religious belief controls behaviour doesn't stand up to close examination, and we don't always act as our belief-systems tell us to or imply that we should!

2. *Is environmental damage confined to or worse in Christian cultures?*

White assumes that serious damage to the environment first appeared in Christian medieval Europe, and that since then the worst damage has been concentrated in the Christian West. He has a rather rosy image of a trouble-free ancient Greece and Rome and a damage-free Orient. But to jump from these snapshots to concluding that Christianity is the root cause of the damage is to elevate the circumstantial evidence too far. And it presupposes that the circumstantial evidence is correct!

But the evidence tells a rather different story. Archaeological evidence reveals that environmental damage began in many places at least 10,000 years ago, long before the Bible was written, when prehistoric men started to hunt birds and animals for food, and set fire to forests to clear land for fields and to drive large animals over cliffs (for food). Documentary evidence in the Old Testament describes the destruction of the evergreen cedars and cypresses of which Lebanon was once so proud. The record shows that they were cleared partly by Egyptian Pharaohs and the kings of Assyria or Babylon, who felled the trees for timber to build temples and palaces.

Documentary sources also indicate that the early Greeks and Romans altered their environment a great deal, before the birth of Christ.[13] Forest clearance, overgrazing and soil erosion were common throughout ancient Greece, and large areas were affected by Roman engineering schemes – including the building of bridges over large rivers and roads through high mountains, and the subdivision of land into equal-sized plots for farming. Historic sources also record widespread exploitation and damage of nature by Oriental cultures. Buddhists felled many trees throughout Japan to build huge wooden halls and temples.[14] Ancient Chinese poetry records dense forest in areas which are now treeless, the clearance starting as far back as 300 BC and was caused by the use of wood to make charcoal for industrial fuel and in building the old Chinese cities. The ancient Chinese custom of burning trees to deprive dangerous animals of their hiding places further aggravated the situation. Timber shortage was reported in the southeastern coastal provinces of China from the tenth to the fourteenth centuries, caused mainly by use of wood in funeral pyres for cremation of the dead.[15]

The evidence of serious environmental problems in non-Christian cultures is not confined to historic examples. Vast areas in Eastern Europe and the Soviet Union have been badly damaged by industrial pollution and environmental damage promoted by centrally-planned socialist systems, with no input from religious beliefs whatsoever.

So, the records reveal that environmental problems are not confined to Christian times and areas. None of the major world faiths is entirely innocent, and none is entirely responsible.

3. Did science and technology grow directly from roots in Christianity?

A central thread in White's thesis is the assumption that Christianity had a direct and strong influence on the development of science and technology. But did it?

Many historians of science argue that White's view is too simplistic, and that science and technology evolved in a much more complex way as a result of the interplay of a wide range of factors and forces. It is a false simplification to single out Christianity when many other factors were also at work, like geography, climate, population growth, urbanism, trade and democracy.[16] The origins of Western science and technology are generally believed to be much more multiple, complex and obscure than White allows for.

It is also true that the initial fostering of science, and subsequent control of its development and application are not the same thing. There are grounds for accepting that Christianity had a strong hand to play in the former, but that doesn't necessarily make it guilty of the latter. The real problem seems to lie more with what we do with technology, rather than the fact that technology exists or what forces gave rise to it in the first place. In other words, the problem is really our attitude towards material goods (particularly technological gadgets) which is not unrelated to our attitudes towards nature.

4. Are other factors involved, as well as science and technology?

White assumes that our attitude towards nature provides the motive and our technology provides the means of exploiting and damaging the environment. Critics argue that he grossly over-simplified the situation. History shows that man's mastery over nature (certainly in

Europe)[17] had to await population increase, administrative centralization and the development of new technological skills (such as land drainage). It didn't arise simply as a product of Christian teaching that man has dominion over nature.

Some historians[18] argue that the environmental crisis is more a product of capitalism and modern democracy than of medieval Christianity. The recent history of North America, for example, has seen an initial sense of Puritan restraint and purpose replaced by secular values of pleasure, violence and materialism and the emergence of a lifestyle based on mass production, a throwaway mentality and a perpetual drive for possessions.[19]

5. Does the Bible encourage and endorse an attitude of domination and exploitation of nature?

Perhaps the central tenet of White's argument, and certainly the part which has since been eagerly seized upon by the greens, is the claim that Christian teaching on nature encourages and endorses domination, exploitation, use and damage. White based the claim largely on the instruction from God that man be made in his image to "rule over the fish of the sea and the birds of the air, over the livestock, over all the earth [as in land], and over all the creatures that move along the ground" (Genesis 1:26). But a careful reading of the Bible reveals that far from instructing us to become tyrants, we are to be stewards of the earth and all of its creatures.

Many critics find no biblical basis to support White's argument.[20] The emphasis in fact is just the opposite – on our responsibility for the environment. Part of White's problem seems to be his simplistic and unacceptable interpretation of the two versions of the creation story which appear in Genesis.[21] By blurring them together he partly obscured their meaning and left out some significant elements. The first account (the Priestly or P account) appears mainly in the first chapter of Genesis (Genesis 1:1–2:4a), and is generally dated around the fifth century BC. The second (the YHWH (Jahweh) or J account) appears later (Genesis 2:4b-25) but the text is believed to be earlier (by up to 500 years).

White overlooks the fact that in the J account God made man for the purpose of tilling the soil (Genesis 2:4–7:15) and God made other living beings for the purpose of providing him with fit helpers (Genesis 2:18f), whereas in the P account man and woman were made simultaneously "in the image of God" (Genesis 1:27). He also blurs the sequence of events in the two accounts of creation – happily taking aspects of each and ignoring their basic differences. Moreover, there is no basis in the Bible texts for White's conclusion that all creation was made to serve man's purposes. White's summary totally ignores and omits God's repeated affirmation that he regarded all creatures and all living things as having inherent value, declaring that "God saw everything that he had made, and behold it was good" (Genesis 1:31).

A number of post-White greens, such as English writer John Button,[22] have welcomed what they see as a change of attitude in recent years amongst Jews and Christians towards stewardship rather than domination. Some misguidedly view this as a belated response and a disguised confession of prior guilt by Christians, stimulated by a new ecological awareness.[23] What they forget, or perhaps never realized, is that stewardship has been an established orthodox doctrine throughout Christian history.

*6. Did exploitative attitudes towards nature diffuse
with the spread of Christianity?*

White argues that the relation between man and nature
changed as Christianity spread and eclipsed paganism,
and as more and more people saw nature as there to be
used and exploited rather than worshipped and valued.
But there is little evidence that this happened.[24] Recall,
too, that behaviour only partly depends on belief, and
White offers a non-standard interpretation of what the
Bible teaches about man's proper relationship with
nature.

There is no doubting the argument that Christianity
withdrew the natural world from the realm of worship
and this removed the religious taboos and restrictions of
animism. But this is a good thing not a bad thing![25]

A CHRISTIAN RESPONSE

Lynn White's paper has turned out to be one of the most
influential sources in shaping modern green attitudes.
The so-called "White thesis" is open to questioning on
various grounds, as we have seen. But it continues to be
widely quoted, if only because it fits comfortably onto
the hidden agendas of those green writers who continue
to repeat his line of argument as if it were established
fact.

Despite the obvious problems it has caused – Christianity discredited and the Bible and its teachings dismissed
as the root cause of environmental problems – White's
paper has brought one important benefit. By causing
many people (Christians and non-Christians alike) to
think seriously about the impact of Christian thought on
the understanding of man's relationship to the natural

world, it has raised awareness of the problem and suggested some useful directions to explore.

Christianity is no more and no less to blame in causing or continuing the environmental crisis than other major faiths, or than the secular way of life which is so popular today. There are two ways forward for Christianity – develop a clearer theology of nature (and the environment), and develop more environmentally-acceptable practices. Both point to a positive and immensely practical green Christianity, and both are required without delay.

CHAPTER SIX

SAINTS AND SETTLERS

Critics of Christianity's contribution to the green debate centre on the aggressive attitude to nature which they read into the Genesis account of creation. There is another side to the story, because many phases of Christian history testify to a genuine desire to treat nature properly. But many greens prefer to overlook the environment-friendly Christian figures from the past, as well as the early settlers in the brave new world of North America.

LESSONS FROM THE SAINTS

There are distinct traces of a green Christian heritage in the Bible, in Christian traditions and in the early Saints.[1] Our knowledge of the lives and works of the early Saints is obviously limited and doubtless partisan, but enough remains for us to pick out some notable friends-of-the-earth amongst the saints.

St Brendan of Clonfert (who died in 575), for example, was an explorer who wrote about his great sea-voyage. According to history, the monks who accompanied him made friends out of every creature they met on their travels, taking a particularly keen interest in the sea birds which followed them and in a friendly whale they encountered on the high seas. St Columbanus (who died in 615), a Celt, travelled widely throughout Europe and tried to encourage a respect for nature wherever he went. History speaks of his compassion for nature – the rivers and springs, trees and forests, plants and animals he came into contact with – and there are contemporary reports of him walking prayerfully in the woods and communicating with birds and squirrels (an early forerunner of St Francis of Assisi). St Cuthbert (who died in 687), is also said to have felt a close affinity with animals, and – as seems quite fitting for the British patron saint of conservation – there are tales of him befriending birds.

We also find a sympathetic view of nature in the writings of St Thomas Aquinas (1225–74), the Italian theologian and Dominican friar whose *Summa Theologiae* (1267–73) was the first attempt at a comprehensive theological system. Thomas had a strong sense of God's abiding presence in creation. He encouraged a wider appreciation of the order, variety and beauty of creation, based on Old Testament teachings about order ordained by God within which man is careful guardian. He may have been the first to emphasize Christian stewardship of God's creation.

Three particular saints stand out as giants in the field of man's relationship to nature – Augustine, Francis and Benedict.

St Augustine

Saint Augustine (354–430) was bishop of Hippo in North Africa between 396 and 430 and one of the Fathers of the Christian Church. His preaching and writing – particularly his book *De Civitate Dei* (The City of God) – had a profound and lasting influence on the subsequent development of theology.

Although the main focus of Augustine's theology was

human history and human salvation, it did also encompass the natural world. It had two special hall-marks – an understanding of the universal beauty and goodness of all things, and a rich vision of a gentle but powerful God governing all things.[2] Augustine argued that the perfection and order of the natural world offered a mirror to the glory of God who created and sustains the universe. He believed that nature was created ulti-mately to bring glory to God, but it also served as a blessing for mankind. He also believed that God's care is not confined to spiritual matters, but that he continually governs the whole of his creation, often through creatures within nature.

St Francis

Without doubt the most influential saint, in the context of nature and conservation, was St Francis of Assisi (1181–1226), the Italian monk who founded the Francis-can order of friars.

Heralded by Lynn White himself as "the greatest saint of the Middle Ages"[3], Francis lived a life of poverty, simplicity and humility. His was a joyful and productive life deliberately chosen, not a miserable existence born out of circumstance or tolerated grudgingly. Taking Jesus as his role-model of the ideal man, he saw humility as a virtue and poverty as liberation from the bondage of materialism and self-reliance. Francis believed that he did not own or have rights over any creature[4] and he felt free to simply enjoy nature in an aesthetic rather than a utilitarian way. One of Francis's greatest qualities was his unqualified and seemingly unending love of all cre-ation.[5]

To him nature was interesting and important in its own right. All parts of creation were holy and precious.

In the delicate petals of the smallest flower, in the graceful flight of the tiniest bird, he saw beauty and God's love and care. He even believed that inanimate parts of creation, such as rocks and cliffs, display God's creative power and attention to detail.

Through the poverty which he so freely embraced, Francis was able to establish a new relationship with creation. Legend has it that he used to preach to the birds and the flowers just as he preached to people, hinting at a belief that they too have souls and moral responsibilities. It is even said that he spoke to a wild wolf at Gubbio in northern Italy, convinced it of its sinful ways as an aggressive predator, and the wolf eventually repented.[6]

Francis tried to set up a democracy of all God's creatures within which every creature would have equal status. This, he hoped, would displace man from his self-imposed monarchy over creation. He saw the rest of creation as his fellow creatures (he even describes them as his brothers and sisters, under God's fatherhood), given the same responsibility as man to praise God and glorify him as their creator. It was for this reason that Lynn White heralded Francis as "the greatest revolutionary in history"[7] and proposed him as the patron saint for ecologists.

The Franciscan emphasis on nature as friend and rejection of damaging intervention in nature has since reappeared in various ways, for example in the nature writings of the Romantics and in modern conservation thinking.

St Benedict

St Francis's reverence for nature and reluctance to interfere with what he and his monks (the Greyfriars) and followers saw as God's perfect creation encouraged passive worship of nature. In sharp contrast, St Benedict and his followers saw it as man's duty to be active within creation – working, changing and shaping nature as a practical ingredient in their lives of divine devotion, meditation and worship.

Benedict (?480–?547), an Italian monk, established a monastery on Monte Cassino in Italy in about 540 AD. Conscious of the risk of physical idleness, he ruled that all of the monks should work with their hands in the fields and in shops. The Benedictine rule was derived from the second chapter of Genesis, where God placed man in the Garden of Eden as steward not master. They developed a way of life in which each person used their practical and intellectual skills to the glory of God.[8] The Benedictine view, still dominant today, was that to work is to pray.

The original Benedictines settled on the hills and were encouraged to use their skills in developing technology. They were creative and inventive, developing windmills and watermills as sources of power used to convert farming products into manufactured goods (such as leather, fabrics, paper, even liqueurs such as Benedictine and Chartreuse).

The original Benedictine monasteries were important and highly organized communities, in which the primary goal was learning obedience as a means to self-forgetfulness leading to union with God.[9] The communities were also self-contained and self-sufficient. Benedictine Rule 66 said that, if possible, the monastery is "to be so constituted that all things necessary, such as water, a mill, a garden, and the various crafts may be contained within it".

Microbiologist Rene Dubos prefers Saint Benedict to Saint Francis as a possible patron saint for ecologists, dismissing Francis as "unworldly". As he sees it, "reverence is not enough, because man has never been a passive witness of nature . . . (we need a) willingness to accept responsibility for creative stewardship of the earth".[10] Benedict's monks cleared forests, drained swamps and marshes and tilled the soil.

The Cistercians

Gradually the Benedictine monasteries went into decline, after they became more and more dependent on endowments for their survival and as the gulf widened between them and society at large. From the Benedictine tradition grew a Cistercian reform movement (of White Monks), which was established in 1098 along the lines of the original Benedictine rule but with a greater emphasis on poverty, simplicity and withdrawal.

The Cistercians usually settled in the valleys, and in Britain colonized some of the more remote places of northern England. They established monasteries in wooded river bottoms and marshy lands – waterlogged sites, often infested with malaria, which had been left by earlier settlers. Such inhospitable sites were chosen on purpose, as the Cistercians withdrew to the frontiers of settled society. Their lifestyle was self-sufficient and self-contained.[11]

Many lay helpers assisted them to reclaim waste land, clear woodland and forests, and drain marshes and waterlogged sites to create productive farmland (learning how to control malaria in the process). They preferred sheep to cattle, which helped to fertilize and improve pastures as well as yielding better financial returns.

The Cistercians shared the Benedictine view that the world was in some ways unfinished, and that mankind was created as stewards of nature who are in control but are answerable to the Creator at the end of the day for the good condition of the estate.[12] It is mainly from the Cistercians that the monastic tradition has gained its reputation for ecological sense.

SETTLERS IN THE NEW WORLD

The saints offer many lessons about Christian attitudes towards nature and practical land management and resource conservation. More modern examples of environment-friendly Christian lifestyles and practices include the attempts by religious folk to colonize North America.

Ironically, the settlers who were seeking to establish new ways of living ended up causing widespread damage to their new environments. This happened partly because they saw the taming of nature as a divine duty. But they were also struggling with what were to them strange environments, and few had any real experience of farming and land management to fall back on.

The Puritans

First to arrive were the Pilgrim Fathers, a group of English Puritans who sailed across the Atlantic on the Mayflower to New England, where they founded Plymouth Colony in 1620 (in what is now South East Massachusetts). Many of the early settlers were Puritans – fundamentalist English Protestants, mostly Calvinists who wished to purify the Church of England of the ceremonial aspects which they dismissed as Catholic and irrelevant to the saving of human souls.

The Puritans saw their task as an immensely spiritual one – to settle in a new land and try to establish a proper biblical lifestyle there, untainted by the ceremonial orthodoxy of the home country they left behind. They took with them dreams for a new future, and hopes for a new lifestyle. To them North America was a land of opportunity and abundance, and they saw their exodus very much as God's calling to his chosen ones to occupy a promised land. Thus they felt a certain close affinity to the people of Israel in the Old Testament whose own lengthy exodus took them to the Promised Land of Canaan.

Many of the pioneering settlers in America took the Genesis command to "be fruitful and increase in number; fill the earth and subdue it" (Genesis 1:28) very seriously indeed. In fact they saw it as their God-given duty to convert wilderness into civilization. This licence to "subdue" the earth encouraged them to develop aggressive and profoundly utilitarian attitudes and practices. Reliable accounts survive of Puritan endeavours in colonial New England, which included "assaults upon forests, wildlife, and the soil. Carried on almost like the wars against the Indians, the war against the land resulted in cutting down the big trees, killing much of the furbearing animal population, and exhausting the light cover of topsoil."[13] Many farms failed, because of poor land management and unenlightened husbandry. Before long the colonial landscape was littered with abandoned farmsteads with stone walls and wooden fences enclosing unkept fields and pastures.

A variety of factors help to explain the Puritans' damage of nature in New England, not just their religious beliefs.[14] They were trying to work inhospitable land which had severe natural constraints, including heavy clays. Natural pastureland was in short supply, and the mixed farming and wood-consuming economy of the settlers did not suit the local environment. Understanding of good farming practices was limited, because few of the Puritan immigrants had been farmers in England before they left for the New World.

But there were attempts within the New England colonies to protect wildlife and landscape, even during this era of settlement and exploitation.[15] Each colony passed statutes which made provisions to protect natural resources in the area immediately surrounding the settlements – some restricting the invasion of common fields and pastures by unwelcome livestock (especially hogs), others protecting streams from overfishing and forests from overcutting.

There is no escaping the fact that the Puritans' treatment of nature as there to be used and exploited contributed significantly to the damage of New England. Ironically, the same conclusion applies equally well to our second group of New World settlers – the Mormons. Indeed the New England Puritans shared many environmental beliefs with the Mormons.[16] Both groups based their policy of land distribution on people's ability to develop resources, and allocated agricultural holdings on the basis of family size. Both believed that God, through nature, had provided them with all their needs. Both encouraged thrift. Both introduced conservation laws to protect scarce timber resources. Both tried to establish a land tenure system of agricultural villages with communal grazing lands. Both saw themselves as bound by a covenantal obligation to develop the wilderness and create Zion (the heaven-like city of God on earth, where his elected ones would live) in North America.

The Mormons
After Joseph Smith (who founded the Mormon Church in 1830) was shot dead in 1844, Brigham Young took over

leadership and led the Mormons west, to settle by the Great Salt Basin in Utah. The early Mormons believed that it was their duty to return the earth to the perfect state it had been in the Garden of Eden, starting in Utah. They accepted without question the Old Testament view that land was a vehicle through which God rewarded or punished human behaviour, and believed that one of God's principal means of rewarding the faithful was through gifts of land for them to use.[17] The inhospitable Great Salt Basin was their Promised Land.

The Mormons' task, as they saw it, had three key challenges. They were to redeem the earth from the curse which had fallen on it when Adam first sinned in the Garden of Eden, build a peaceful world in which man and nature lived in happy harmony, and finish God's creation by making the earth even more beautiful than it is naturally by sound farming practices.[18]

By developing the land and extracting resources from it the Mormons believed that they were redeeming the earth from its curse as well as establishing a means of subsistence. Like the Puritans, the Mormons' practices caused widespread damage to the environment even though they had a favourable environmental theology and genuinely believed they were following God's instructions. The landscape of Utah still shows much evidence of over-grazing, deep gulleys on steep slopes caused by felling of trees, salinization (high salt concentrations) and waterlogging of irrigated desert soils.[19] Some of the damage can be attributed to their zealous taming of nature, and some to their lack of understanding of the peculiarities of this harsh desert environment (they were, after all, used to the temperate environments of the Mid-West and northern Europe).

PART THREE

GREEN THEOLOGY

CHAPTER SEVEN

TOWARDS A THEOLOGY OF NATURE

Most of the debate over Christianity as the root cause of the environmental crisis ignores what the Bible actually says about nature, so it is important to examine this and try to set it into context. But the task of developing such a theology is not an easy one, for various reasons.

For a start, the Bible wasn't written for that purpose and there are obvious dangers of reading too much into passages which mention nature, when that is incidental to the main theme or purpose of the passage.[1] We have to dig deep to find relevant material and be extremely careful how we interpret it. We are unlikely to learn much, for example, either from isolated proof tests or from the lack of definitive statements. What's more most of the texts which directly mention the natural world and its creatures are in the Old Testament, so they predate Jesus and his ministry on earth.[2]

There is also the danger of transplanting ancient institutions, customs and practices directly into today's society.[3] There are no biblical texts which deal specifically with many modern environmental issues and problems, such as toxic waste disposal, and it is wrong to expect that we will find explicit examples of how to cope with them in scripture. Traditional Judaism has nothing to say about our environmental crisis – in fact, there isn't even a word for *nature* in rabbinic Hebrew.[4]

A theology of nature must extend beyond the simplistic conclusion that the only message the Bible offers about use of environment is that Adam was told to "subdue the earth".

A framework

The Bible suggests at least three ways in which man interacts with nature.[5] One is based on the belief that human rights take precedence over nature's rights, and it sees man as an overlord. The second sees man as nature's caretaker and a creative steward of the earth, preserving wholeness and the unity of creation. A third views man as a wondering onlooker amazed by nature as God's handiwork, overflowing with miracles, mystery and majesty.

MAN AS A WONDERING ONLOOKER

Why should we protect nature and use it wisely? It goes without saying that nature provides us with all of our material needs – food, water, shelter, resources to manufacture other things from. These utilitarian needs and benefits are obvious. But nature offers us other benefits too.

Nature is something which inspires us, and we appreciate it. Through nature we appreciate the inherent worthiness of things and of their creator. Our emotions are often moved in a powerful way simply by looking at a spectacular view (such as the Grand Canyon) or attractive wildlife (such as exotic birds). The concept of nature portrayed in the Psalms (such as 93 and 104) points to a beautiful and awe-inspiring natural world which has value because it shows God's wisdom and power in its existence and the way it works.[6]

Nature is also an education. Some Bible passages encourage us to draw lessons for our own lives from the ways of nature. The ant, for example, gathers enough food at harvest time to see it through lean times; there are lessons here for lazy people about forward planning (Proverbs 6: 6–8). Nature also teaches us about ethics and caring for other people and things. The birds and flowers are good examples of parts of creation which meet God's expectations for them (Matthew 6:26–30), so they offer a moral and religious example to man.

Nature also stimulates faith in God. Recall the medieval view of nature as a book of divine revelation, a window to God. If nature is the product of God's creative handiwork, and he is permanently overseeing and controlling it, then we should be able to see something of him in it (Psalm 19:1, Isaiah 42:5, Romans 1:19–20).

A theology of nature must reflect these inherent values within nature, which is not there simply for us to use and abuse as we see fit. But it must also take into account why God created nature, and how man's self-centred behaviour has effectively put it under God's curse.

_____ **CREATION** _____

The creation of the earth and everything in it is described in Genesis. We must view the creation story in the sense in which it was written – with the emphasis on *why* God created (which is the domain of theology) rather than on *how* he did it (the domain of science).

There are two primary concerns in the Genesis creation accounts[7] – to emphasize the dependence of all of creation on God, and to describe the order God established within creation.

Creation by God

The earth and everything in it were created by God, and they belong to him (Genesis 1:1). If only for this reason creation has intrinsic worth. What's more, God created it all from nothing (Genesis 1:2). It happened by his word; he gave the earth shape, function and meaning simply by instruction. He commanded and creation responded.

The earth becomes progressively more orderly and more habitable as each scene of the creation drama unfolds.[8] Night is separated from day; sky is separated from land; vegetation covers the earth; sun, moon and stars appear; seas and sky are filled with wildlife; man is created. At the end of this work of creation God rested.

The Sabbath marks the crowning glory of this divine act of creation, when the designer and creator could rest and reflect on it all. The creation narratives paint the picture of a powerful God with a clear sense of purpose behind what he was creating.

God created the universe complete. Nothing necessary was left out, and nothing unnecessary was put in. He created wholeness and harmony within nature (Psalm 136:25, Job 39, Psalm 104). This does not necessarily mean there is no room for natural change within nature, such as the extinction of some species and the emergence of new ones. But it does mean that the natural world must be seen in its entirety, as a complex and highly interactive and interrelated system, not just a set of bits and pieces.

Dependence, judgment and thanksgiving

The creation passages also reveal a God with a keen interest in detail. But this was no one-off burst of enthusiasm centred on the initial act of creation. It was to be an enduring and sustained endeavour. The important theme of all things depending on God appears repeatedly through the Bible (for example in Psalm 24:1 and Isaiah 40:28).

God liked the world he created, and was pleased with what he had made. After each part of the universe was created "God saw that it was good" (Genesis 1:10, 1:12, 1:18, 1:21, 1:25). What's more, he liked all of his creation (Genesis 1:31), not just the separate parts. This gives to nature a derived dignity[9] which complements its inherent value.

God's pleasure with his handiwork is not the only sign that he passed judgment over his creation. He went further and blessed all the living things he had created, instructing them to "be fruitful and increase in number" (Genesis 1:22). This blessing also extended to people (Genesis 1:28).

The whole of creation is called upon to praise God, its creator and sustainer. Nature, like man, is repeatedly told throughout the Old Testament to praise God and rejoice. The Psalms in particular are a rich source of such nature texts (Psalm 148: 3–10, Psalm 150: 6, Psalm 65: 12–13, Isaiah 55:12, 1 Chronicles 16:23–33).

THE RISE OF MAN

The crowning glory of God's creation was man. Adam, the first human, was created by God as a perfect individual (Genesis 1:26-7). He was set in a perfect world where everything worked properly, everything was where it belonged, everything had all its needs met, and everything was part of a harmony and peaceful co-existence the like of which we have not seen since.

Man, like the animals, was also blessed by God and instructed to "be fruitful and increase in number" (Genesis 1:28). Both man and the animals were created by God's Holy Spirit (Psalm 104:30), and both were created from the dust on the ground (Genesis 2:7 and 19). Yet God created man separately to and different from the rest of creation. Man's uniqueness stems from the fact that God created him to be like God (Genesis 1:26; Psalm 8:4–5).

Subdue the earth

Man's creation was also unique because he was commanded by God to "subdue" the rest of creation, to "rule over the fish of the sea and the birds of the air and over every living creature that moves on the ground" (Genesis 1:28).

This command was not an afterthought. As the very first thing that God says to the people he had created, it must have been a high priority for God and thus for man too. And because God had given the instruction, responsibility for subduing the earth and ruling over the creatures is not one that man has taken on himself. This is not the same as saying that the rest of creation was made for man. Nowhere does the Bible say that nature was created for man's benefit.

The creation account in Genesis 2 gives two particular clues to what this command to "subdue" the earth was intended to mean. The first is that God placed Adam "in the Garden of Eden to work it and take care of it" (verse 15). This hints at a relationship between God and man similar to that between a tenant farmer (man) and the estate owner (God). The verb *abad* in verse 15 implies service as well as work; man was placed in Eden by God's power to serve and preserve the earth on God's behalf. The second clue is that God told man to name the creatures (verses 19–20). It is difficult to imagine God trusting man to select names for each creature if he did not also trust man to take care of them on his behalf.

THE FALL OF MAN

The earth was created perfect, but things were to change when Adam committed the original sin in the Garden of Eden (Genesis 3:1–14).

In the Fall, man breaks his unique relationship with God who pronounces his punishment via a curse on people and nature (Genesis 3:14–24). Nature becomes an enemy to man (verse 17), man is cursed with hard physical labour (18–19) and Adam is expelled from the Garden of Eden "to work the ground from which he had been taken" (Genesis 3:23). All of nature is cursed by the Fall of Man (Genesis 3:17). This is confirmed in the New Testament (Romans 8:19–21). Nature has paid the price for man's selfish behaviour.

THE FLOOD

God's patience with the humans he had created, who were becoming more and more self-centred and wicked, and less and less obedient, was not limitless (Genesis 6:6), so he sent "the flood" (described in Genesis 6) to wipe out most of creation. The only exceptions were

Noah and his family, and the creatures he saved in the ark (verse 7). After the flood waters subsided, God decided to make a new beginning for all creatures (Genesis 9:8–11).

After the flood God turns the clock back for his creation and allows it a second start. God's second covenant with man (the first was with Adam and Eve in the Garden of Eden) was made with Noah and his family who survived the flood. God repeats his commandment to Noah and his family to "Be fruitful and increase in number and fill the earth" (Genesis 9:1). He also puts man in charge of all the creatures and commands them be fruitful and increase in number (Genesis 8:17). In this new covenant, which is to be everlasting, God promises never again to curse the ground because of man or to destroy all living creatures (Genesis 8:21–2). He designates the rainbow as a reminder of this new covenant (Genesis 9:12–16).

THE EXODUS AND THE PROMISED LAND

The links between God, man and nature continue through the Old Testament, starting with the journey of the Israelites towards the Promised Land. God promised Abraham that his descendants would become God's chosen people (Genesis 12:2) and he promised them the land of Canaan as an everlasting home (Genesis 12:7), although it would be over six centuries before they would finally occupy it.

God used nature in various ways to help the people of Israel in their great escape from slavery in Egypt (Exodus 1–18). The King of Egypt was attacked with nine plagues including frogs, gnats, flies, animal disease, hail, locusts and darkness (Exodus 7–10) to force him to release them.

The waters of the Red Sea were parted to let through the fleeing Israelites before the Egyptian army (Exodus 14). God provided manna (bread) and quail for them when they were crossing the desert (Exodus 16), and provided water from a rock (Exodus 17:1–7).

When they eventually arrived in Canaan – the long awaited Promised Land – with Joshua now in charge, the Israelites had to conquer it and take it from the people who were already living there (Joshua 1–8). Each of the twelve tribes of Israel was then given its own land to settle on (Joshua 13–21).

JESUS CHRIST

Because man continued to sin, God demonstrated his love by sending his son Jesus Christ to earth to live as a man and to die on a cross (John 3:16). Through the death and resurrection of Jesus God provides the means for each person to re-establish a proper relationship with God, by forgiveness of their sins (Romans 8:1, Romans 4:25). The apostle Paul describes graphically how the person who believes in Jesus "is a new creation; the old has gone, the new has come!" (2 Corinthians 5:17).

God's plan was not completed with the ascension into heaven of Jesus. Jesus referred to his second coming as the "renewal of all things" (Matthew 19:28). His return will allow everything God originally created to be recreated with inherent qualities of goodness, wholeness and perfection restored in them (Colossians 1:17, 20 and Ephesians 1:10). When Jesus returns all of creation, including nature, will be released from the curse God imposed on it after Adam sinned (Romans 8:19–22).

DOMINION

A central theme throughout the Bible is dominion, meaning rule or authority. Sometimes it refers to ruling over creation, and sometimes it refers to God ruling over mankind. The word first appears in Genesis 1:28, which the King James version translates as "have dominion over". The New International Version prefers "rule over", and the Good News Bible talks of "putting in charge of".

The idea of dominion over nature appears in the Bible in two senses – dominion by God and dominion by man.

DOMINION BY GOD

God's dominion over the earth is derived from his role as creator, expressed in his role as sustainer and controller, and justified by his role as owner. As we are reminded, "the earth is the Lord's, and everything in it" (Psalm 24:1).

Everything he created has value (even if it is not always financial or utilitarian), everything has purpose (even if we can't work out what it is), and everything belongs (even if we don't always think so).[10]

But God continues to be interested in, care for and assume ultimate control of his creation. This does not mean that the original creation was in any way deficient and needs to be repaired. It does mean that he is intimately involved in every little detail of it, every second of the day.

A recurrent theme in the Bible is the balance between God as sovereign over nature (transcendent), yet also active within it (immanent). God is *in* the world but not *of* it; within and without, simultaneously. We see this, for example, in his concern for nature after the Flood (Genesis 9:8–17), for every bird and animal (Psalm 50:10–12) and for people on a daily basis (Matthew 6:26–30). We see it, too, in God's control of the elements – earthquakes and volcanoes (Psalm 18:7–8), the sea and waves, the seasonal rains and harvest times (Jeremiah 5:22–3), powerful storms (Psalm 77:18) and thunder (Psalm 29, Psalm 18:13), snow and ice (Psalm 147:15–18). God provides rain to produce grain, wine and oil, and grass to feed the cattle (Deuteronomy 11:10–17).

A recurrent theme in the Old Testament is the way God uses nature as a reward for people's obedience and a punishment for their disobedience (see, for example, Deuteronomy 11:13–17).

Divine punishment comes, for example, in the plagues of Egypt and the destruction of Sodom and Gomorrah. Divine provision includes the fertile and bountiful Promised Land (Deuteronomy 8:7–10), as well as animals to help faithful people who are in trouble – such as Jonah and the whale (Jonah 2:1–10), and Daniel in the lion's den (Daniel 6:21–3).

This divine environmental "carrot and stick" has profound implications for a theology of nature, because it means that such a theology must extend way beyond simply caring for plants and animals. It must accommodate the wider issues of human behaviour, even when that behaviour is not even directed at nature.

So, everything in the material world was created by God, is dependent on him for continued existence and belongs to him. It is not God, but it bears his imprint. It is not to be worshipped, but it is blessed and loved by God. A theology of nature should make such considerations explicit.

DOMINION BY MAN

Many green writers criticize Christianity's view of nature for being exploitative and damaging. The basis of this argument is the Genesis account of creation which speaks of God creating man, instructing him to be fruitful and to rule over the other creatures.

The Genesis account paints a clear picture of God creating man as the head of all living things, to govern the earth and to use its resources responsibly. Man's dominion over nature was a gift from God. The stated human task at creation was earthkeeping (Genesis 2:15). But, some argue, this responsibility was soon abused as men started to exploit and overuse nature.

The so-called "despotism school" views Genesis 1:26–8 as a mandate for tyrannical human control over nature. But the notion of unequal status was built into God's creation, because hierarchies are inherent in nature.[11] The sun rules the day and the moon rules the night (Genesis 1:16), the sea monster Leviathan apparently rules the sea (Job 41:1–34) and Behemoth (possibly the hippopotamus) rules the world of land animals (Job 40:15–24). God rules the whole. Thus man's assumed position of superiority over the rest of creation would not be breaking entirely new ground.

But the question of whether the Genesis passages excuse a despotic attitude towards nature really depends on the original meanings of the texts, not on modern translations of them.[12] The two key verbs are *radah* (generally translated as "to have dominion over" or "rule") and *kabas* (generally translated as "subdue").

Jewish scholars see in *radah* a meaning similar to that of a king ruling over an area, with a responsibility to maintain order and harmony.[13] Dominion in this sense implies the subordination of the rest of creation under man (who is made like but not equal to God), rather than some divine licence for man to oppress and destroy it.

The word *kabas* poses a problem, too, because in the other contexts in which it is used throughout the Old Testament it implies violence.[14] The same word is used for rape (Esther 7:8), forcing people into slavery (2 Chronicles 28:10) and conquering people and lands in war (Joshua 18:1). But in the context in which it is used in Genesis, it corresponds to working or tilling of the ground (as in Genesis 2:5 and 15).

The emphasis in Genesis does not appear to lie on man's power or his exploitative activities. The "dominion" argument appears to have been seriously overplayed and understudied, particularly by those outside the Judeo-Christian tradition who wrongly claim to have uncovered the root cause of the environmental crisis. We need to look elsewhere for clues about how to treat the environment. The most promising places to start are by looking at the lessons from the Promised Land and from traditional Jewish views on the stewardship of nature.

LESSONS FROM THE OLD TESTAMENT

There is no doubt that many people in the Old Testament had a good appreciation of the need to use nature wisely, if only because it would serve their needs better if they did. Some of the lessons they learned, doubtless through generations of getting it wrong as well as through direct guidance from God, are just as relevant for us today as they were all those thousands of years ago.

We find some guidelines to sound resource management in the Bible, such as the need to look after herds and rotate stock grazing in the fields (Proverbs 27:23–7). The dangers of overgrazing were well known, as Abram and Lot (Genesis 13:6) and Jacob and Esau (Genesis 36:7) testify. Farmers and shepherds were aware of the need to prevent livestock from polluting springs and water supplies (Ezekiel 34:18–19 and Genesis 29:2–8).

But whilst illustrations like these show that stewardship was not uncommon amongst Old Testament peoples, we really need a much more systematic way of appreciating what the Old Testament has to teach us about managing nature. The Israelites' Exodus to and subsequent inhabitation of the Promised Land offers some valuable lessons.

THE PROMISED LAND

Detailed studies of the ways the early Jewish peoples managed land and nature, particularly during and just after the six centuries of the Exodus during which Judaism was established, have discovered that they had a remarkably enlightened and sustainable set of practices.[15] This was motivated by three things – reverence for the world as God's handiwork, a view of the Land of Israel as sacred, and a belief in the responsibility of society to ensure the safety and comfort of man who is created in the image of God.[16]

As well as figuring so prominently in the history of the Jewish peoples, the whole idea of God giving the Promised Land to the Israelites has some significant implications for how man should relate to nature today. This story may be more relevant to the environmental crisis than the story of the Garden of Eden, because the Promised Land is a divine gift to a *fallen* people.[17]

Fundamental principles

Some basic principles underlie the way the Israelites viewed the Promised Land[18] and these are highly useful reminders of how we should treat nature today.

1. *It is a gift;* because those who possess it did not create it. Moses reminded the Israelites that it is God who gives them the ability to produce wealth (Deuteronomy 8:17–18). This is just as true today.

2. *It is not a permanent gift;* because it belongs to God and is given to us only for a time, and only for so long as it is properly used. Moses reminded his people time and time again that everything they had was God's (Deuteronomy 10:14). God has made man the tenant not the outright owner of the earth, and we are given rights of habitation and use which reflect this. God instructed Moses on Mount Sinai to tell the Israelites "the land must not be sold permanently, because the land is mine and you are but aliens and my tenants" (Leviticus 25:23).

3. God is *landlord* and he dictates the rules; God imposes limits of human control and requires regular periods of rest for the land – a sabbath every seventh year in which fields were to be left fallow, a year of jubilee every fiftieth year during which fields would lie fallow and the land would be returned to its original owners.

4. God *continually cares* for the Promised Land; Moses also reminds his people that it is a land God cares for (Deuteronomy 11:12). God cares for his creation so much that he has promised ultimately to repossess it and repair its perfect form (Romans 8:20–1).

5. *The gift is not given as a reward;* the people chosen

to receive the gift of the Promised Land do not deserve it because they have been faithless and wicked. This creates a moral predicament for them, because having failed to deserve it beforehand, they must prove worthy of it afterwards. If they do not use it properly, it could be taken away from them.[18]

Conditions of the tenancy

If the Promised Land (or in the more general sense nature) is a gift from God to people who do not really deserve it, how can they prove themselves worthy of it? God grants the tenancy on three conditions.

First, the tenants are required to be faithful, grateful and humble. It is their responsibility to remember that the land is a gift. Moses reminded them "When you have eaten and are satisfied, praise the Lord your God for the good land he has given you." (Deuteronomy 8:10).

Second, they must be neighbourly and honest. This means being fair and just, kind to one another, generous to strangers and honest in transactions. It is neighbourly for us to preserve the land for those who follow us, because it is an inheritance not a possession.

Third, those who receive the gift are expected to practise good husbandry and look after it on behalf of its ultimate owner. We shall consider below what this meant in practice for the resource managers in the Old Testament.

The theme which underlies most of the Bible passages dealing with the Promised Land is man as steward or tenant of God's created world. God (the owner) gives man (the tenant) responsibility to look after it on his behalf until the time comes for God to come and transform it completely. Man is also given fairly clear guidance on how he should look after it.

EXERCISE OF STEWARDSHIP: THE JEWISH VIEW

There are many references throughout the Old Testament to man's stewardship of creation, especially of the land itself. It is possible to fit together the main pieces of a rich and complex jigsaw which portrays the Jewish view of stewardship, derived from the Bible and from Jewish scholarship, tradition and legal sources.[19]

Ownership and accountability

The exercise of stewardship is governed ultimately by a keen awareness of God's ownership of creation and man's responsibility to him for the protection of it. The Jewish scriptures are unambiguous about the relationship between man and God, distinguishing between God as creator and owner of the earth (Deuteronomy 10:14 and Psalm 24:1) and man as its humble caretaker or steward (Genesis 2:15 and Leviticus 25:23). So although God created the earth and appointed mankind to rule over it and to use all its produce for sustenance (Genesis 1: 28–30), everything in the world still belongs to God.

God chose mankind to be resident caretakers of his creation. This was a tremendous privilege. But with it came the responsibility of looking after God's earthly estate. The notion of accountability to God is implicit in both the biblical description of God's gift of creation to man and the image that rabbis had of "the good person".[20]

Laws and rules

The practical outworking of stewardship against this overriding sense of ownership and accountability was also governed by a number of specific rules (a sort of Steward's Manual) which set out man's responsibilities for his behaviour towards all parts of nature. Some were derived from traditional Jewish legal material, the so-called halakhic sources.[21]

The three most important rules, which form the core of the Jewish Steward's Manual, are concerned with destruction of nature, conduct towards animals, and human restraint.

1. Do not destroy

This rule derives from the Hebrew *bal tashhit* which means "do not destroy" (the literal meaning is "you shall not wantonly destroy"). It is borrowed from a set of instructions on how to make war which appear in Deuteronomy – "When you lay siege to a city for a long time, fighting against it to capture it, do not destroy its trees by putting an axe to them, because you can eat their fruit. Do not cut them down. Are the trees of the field people, that you should besiege them? However, you may cut down trees that you know are not fruit trees and use them to build siege works until the city at war with you falls" (Deuteronomy 20:19–20).

This passage provides the basis for the more general rule which governs man's attitude toward nature. The rabbis took this to mean that any destructive activity is forbidden, and this was interpreted broadly. It was an entirely negative rule, stating what is not allowed but offering no positive guidance or encouragement.

All manner of activities were forbidden, including the cutting off of water supplies to trees, overgrazing of the countryside, the unjustified killing of animals or feeding them harmful foods, hunting of animals for sport, extinction of species and destruction of cultivated plant varieties, pollution of air and water, overconsumption of anything and waste of mineral and other resources.

The rule was restrictive because it applied to everybody. Thus it was as grave an offence to destroy nature on one's own property as it was to damage or destroy nature on a neighbour's land.[22]

2. Pain of living things

This rule also dictated what is not permitted. In this case people were not allowed to inflict *za'ar baalei hayyim*, which translates as "pain of living things". The rule governs the human treatment of animals, in essence forbidding inhumane conduct towards animals.

The Old Testament references are very specific. It was forbidden, for example, to take a mother bird from a nest with her young (Deuteronomy 22:6–7). A cow or sheep was not to be slaughtered for sacrifice at the same time as its young, and a young animal was not to be taken from its mother before it was seven days old (Leviticus 22:27–8). A farmer was forbidden to plough with an ox and a donkey yoked together, because it would impose great hardship on the weaker animal (Deuteronomy 22:10). An ox was not to be muzzled while it was treading out the corn (Deuteronomy 25:4).

Although these might appear at first sight to be rather idiosyncratic cases which lack more universal relevance, there is clearly an underlying concern for the physical and emotional state of the animals concerned. As some have pointed out, the ultimate extension of this particular rule is to abstain from killing animals at all. This is one defence of vegetarianism, which has long appealed to Jews although it is not required by Jewish law.

3. Human restraint

The third area of concern, not explicitly a rule, was awareness of the need for restraint and sensitivity in the exercise of human power. A number of general guidelines for practical land management, which also impose some restraint in stewardship, appear in the Old Testament.

For instance, taking care of one's animals is both humane and productive (Proverbs 27: 23–7). When harvesting the crops, the owner of the field was to reap in such a way that something was left for others without resources of their own, including his neighbours and other creatures (Leviticus 23:22).

Such guidelines are practical and doubtless very effective. They encourage sustainable forms of land management, and enable the production of surplus food and raw materials which can be given to the poor and the needy. They also seek to promote a humane attitude towards the whole of creation, in which man and nature are working together in partnership in a mutually advantageous co-operative venture.

THANKSGIVING

Practical issues were also dealt with in the laws of tithing and of gleaning, which recognize God's goodness and continuing provision.

The tithe

The law of tithing recognizes that everything which the land produces – grain, fruit, animals – ultimately belongs to God (Leviticus 27:30–3, Numbers 18:21–32, Deuteronomy 12:5–18, Deuteronomy 14:22–9). One tenth of all produce from the land was to be set aside as a gift for God's provision. The people of Israel were instructed to eat the tithe of grain, new wine and oil, along with the firstborn of the herds and flocks in the presence of God, with thanksgiving and rejoicing.

The law also required that a food reserve be built up every three years, and then given to the Levites (who had no land of their own), to local widows and the fatherless and homeless. Doing this would ensure that God continued to bless their work and their fields.

Tithing was a powerful affirmation of stewardship which recognized that everything we have belongs to God and makes compassionate provision for the disadvantaged.[23]

The law of gleaning

The law of gleaning also recognized the need to look after the poor, by a form of land management which encouraged a sharing of resources (Leviticus 19:9–10, Deuteronomy 24:19–21). It required that the harvests in the fields were not to be reaped to the very edge or the remnants collected afterwards. Neither were the vineyards or olive groves to be stripped bare.

Some produce – the crops in the field corners and edges, that which had fallen during harvesting, the grapes and olives which had fallen to the ground and those which were left on the branches after the first collection – would be left for the poor and the homeless (thus sharing resources).

Again, God would bless the works and land of faithful believers who honoured his law and shared their resources with the poor and the needy. Incidentally, the practice of gleaning doubtless had conservation value as well, because the spared areas would be useful refuges for wildlife.

THE SABBATH

Practical and spiritual issues converge most fully in the Jewish custom of allowing (indeed, *instructing*) man and nature to rest on a regular basis – every seventh day, every seventh year and every fiftieth year.

The Sabbath Day

Perhaps the most important element in the cycle of Jewish activities is the weekly Sabbath, a day of rest. It owes its origins to the day of rest which God took after he "had finished the work he had been doing; on the seventh day he rested from all his work. And God blessed the seventh day and made it holy, because on it he rested from all the work of creating that he had done" (Genesis 2:2–3).

Moses instructed the Israelites to set aside the Sabbath Day each week as a holy day on which they should rest from work and think of God. He told them "the seventh day is a Sabbath to the Lord your God. On it you shall not do any work, neither you, nor your son or daughter, nor your manservant or maidservant, nor your animals, nor the alien within your gates" (Exodus 20:10).

As well as the spiritual benefit of suspending busy routines for one day a week to reflect on higher matters, setting aside the Sabbath also has profound practical implications for nature. Limiting human work and activities also restricts our ability and opportunity to change nature, whilst the Sabbath also allows periods of rest for domesticated animals (Exodus 23:12). So God, man and nature all gain if the Sabbath Day is taken seriously.

Setting aside a weekly day of rest must be seen as a positive not a negative step. The traditionally observant Jew does more than rest, pray and refrain from ordinary work (which are all highly relevant to stewardship) on the Sabbath. He creates nothing, destroys nothing and enjoys the bounty of the earth. In this way the Sabbath becomes a celebration of our tenancy and stewardship in the world.[24] The Sabbath is thus a releasing not a restricting day.

The Sabbatical Year

The Sabbath idea of six days of work followed by a day of rest is mirrored in the Jewish belief that the land should rest and lie fallow every seventh year. The basis of this Sabbatical Year was spelled out by God to Moses on Mount Sinai (Leviticus 25: 3–7, see also Exodus 23:10–11).

The land which God gave to the Israelites could be harvested for six years – the fields sown, vineyards pruned and crops gathered – but every seventh year it was to be allowed to lie fallow, as a "sabbath of rest". Every seventh year the fields were not to be sown or reaped or the vineyards pruned or harvested. This was not to be a time of hardship and misery; everyone's basic need for food – the family, their servants and hired workers – would be met by whatever grew naturally on the land during the seventh year. Even wild animals were to be cared for by letting them have what was left in fields and orchards.

The tough regulations forbid commercial transactions on a large scale. The crop must be used for its natural ends – fruit is to be eaten, juices drunk, oil to anoint human bodies. Such regulations emphasize the sacred character of the natural products in the seventh year, which reminds everyone of God's continuing care and provision.

The Sabbatical Year laws demand an equalization of

all who live off the land and dismantle the notion of private ownership (of land and other resources).[25] Man is allowed to eat what he has stored only as long as God's natural storage (the open fields) hold their crops. He must release the grain he has stored when the wild animals can no longer find food. This provides a vivid reminder that man must live according to the rhythms of nature, despite his obvious ability to circumvent them using technology.

The principal lesson from this idea of a sacred Sabbatical Year is that we are allowed to use God's gifts for our daily needs, but no more. Nature is not to be exploited for greed or profit. In the law of the Sabbatical Year God was reminding people that he owns the land, and they are simply his temporary custodians.[26]

The Year of Jubilee

An even more graphic reminder that all land and all of nature belong ultimately to God comes with the notion of a Year of Jubilee every fiftieth year (Leviticus 25:8–55). The Israelites were instructed to consecrate that year and "proclaim liberty throughout the land to all its inhabitants" (verse 10). That year, too, each Israelite was to "return to his family property and each to his own clan" (verse 10). They were only to eat what came directly from the land; there was to be no sowing or reaping (verses 11–12).

The most important clauses in the Jubilee regulations concern the ownership of land. God reminded the Israelites that "the land must not be sold permanently, because the land is mine and you are but aliens and my tenants. Throughout the country that you hold as a possession, you must provide for the redemption of the land" (verses 23–4). Land was to be returned to its original owner if it was originally sold because of poverty (verses 25–8), and houses in villages without walls round them could also be redeemed and were to be returned in the Year of Jubilee (verse 31).

The Jubilee laws were a powerful reminder that no one had unconditional rights over the land, which belonged to God.

STEWARDSHIP

Genesis 1:26–8 lies at the heart of the debate over Christianity and environment. Ironically, the despot school championed by Lynn White and the stewardship school favoured by Christians both interpret this same passage in almost diametrically opposing ways. Both schools agree that the passage sets mankind slightly outside and above nature, but they disagree fundamentally about whether this dominion is to be arrogant or responsible. The Christian interpretation is that we have an obligation to God to act responsibly, as trustees or stewards.

Trusteeship

A trustee is someone to whom the legal title to property is entrusted to hold or use for another person's benefit. It can be argued that this is precisely the role God has created for people, as trustees of his natural creation on his behalf.

We are beneficiaries not owners of the earth. This implies that in some ways God has made us his special partners, intending that we should be the instrument for fulfilling his sovereignty over creation.[27] By allowing man to name the animals and instructing him to "subdue the earth'', God is challenging us to be co-creators with him, responsible to some extent for the future of nature.[28]

This implied partnership with God is the ultimate privilege for man. But it brings with it unprecedented responsibility to exercise that creative power properly. This means that we should be neither neutral or exploitive, but productive and protective. The purpose and end result of our use of creation must be good, just as God's creation is itself good.[29] We therefore cannot avoid our responsibility, to both God and other people (who are also his partners), to preserve and protect nature.

As trustee of God's estate on earth, man is responsible to its owner for its safe keeping, stability and survival. Causing damage to nature, overexploitation of resources and radical changes to the environment are simply not compatible with the responsibilities of being trustees.

Principles of stewardship

Acting as stewards of God's creation means working within the rules set by God. Man's autonomy to do as he pleases also has limits which are set by God.

These rules or guiding principles are apparent in a number of ways. One, is that God retains ownership of the earth. We are his stewards or tenants, much like a tenant farmer who has temporary custody of a property and must one day hand it over to others. On that day the tenant must account for his actions while the property was in his care. This was the meaning of the Sabbatical Year and Jubilee Year in the law given to Moses.

A second principle is that stewardship is a gift from God, not an achievement of man. It is man's privilege and responsibility to look after God's earth on his behalf. The gift is always conditional on God's provision, and it can be taken back just as easily as it was given. No amount of good work by mankind (for example, no amount of conservation work, no matter how genuine and well-intended this might be) will alter the fact that the role is a gift.

A third principle, often overlooked, is that stewardship is a gift to man collectively, not to individual men. Attempts to monopolize land and other resources for private gain are clear (but common) violations of the underlying rule.

Principle four is that man, unlike God, does not create *de novo* (from nothing) . . . he works with pre-existing things. Thus, for example, in taking responsibility for naming the animals on God's behalf, Adam was very much working with givens. Man works within the limits of a created order with its own pre-existing character.[30]

When we try to create *de novo*, using our brightest brains and our best science and technology, we are still reshaping the material that God created for us. Genetic engineering and nuclear power, perhaps the two most prominent of our recent attempts to radically alter God's created order, are based ultimately on re-ordering what already exists.

A fifth principle is that man must honour the integrity of the pre-existing material. It was, after all, created by God who made it good. Thus responsible human use of the environment must take into account the balances and harmonies of the natural world.

This leads naturally to a sixth principle, that man is always answerable to God. Our freedom to "subdue" is always limited, and under a higher authority (God). Dominion in the Old Testament sense does not mean the right to pollute, oppress and destroy. Human dominion over the rest of nature was, from the start, to be strictly controlled by God.

Principle seven is that man must exercise authority over the rest of creation on behalf of God and with responsibility. We are stewards not owners of the earth, and we have a fundamental obligation to administer God's creation wisely.[31] The responsibility is to care for the earth on behalf of its owner (God). This allows him to use nature for his own needs but does not allow him to destroy it since it is entrusted to him for a limited period. A useful analogy is a book borrower in a library, who is entitled and expected to make the best use of its contents but trusted to handle the books properly so that they are available to others.[32]

An eighth principle is that our stewardship of nature should reflect the "good shepherd" model for which there is ample support in the Bible. Such a shepherd is totally responsible for the welfare of his flock but exercises full authority over them at the same time.[33] Jesus is the exemplary model (Luke 12:42–8).

In final analysis, having the basis for a theology of nature is just the starting point for a serious rethink of how green Christianity should be. Such a theology might guide our attitudes and provide a context for a wider reflection on where modern society appears to be heading.

CHAPTER EIGHT

A CHRISTIAN WAY FORWARD

Most people agree that the world is in a mess and that we have created that mess. On those two basic facts we would all agree. It is after that the disagreements start! Christians and secular greens part company on the question of *why* we have the crisis. What caused it?

The secular view is that the environmental crisis is a *material* problem, stemming from our overuse of resources, unwise reliance on economics, creation of pollution and wastes, and so on. A material problem requires a practical solution. But Christians, and indeed most of the other major world faiths, see it as more of a spiritual problem stemming from our attitudes and values. A spiritual problem requires a *spiritual* solution.

This is not to say that our habits and practices are not a key part of the problem, they obviously are. But the spiritual problem (man's relationship to God, to nature and to his fellow men) is manifest through material symptoms. To change the latter without tackling the former is akin to treating someone's emotional problems by surgery.

Some writers see a direct link between lack of faith and damaging attitudes and behaviour.[1] As a result, instead of turning our minds to higher spiritual things we focus on material things – we value economic growth in itself, rely on technology and need to produce and display our wealth.

Why should Christians be interested?

There is an argument that, since Christians believe Jesus will ultimately return to earth to claim and redeem all of God's creation, they should not be too concerned about the state of the world today. But having our eyes fixed firmly on the future does not mean that we can ignore the present.

Christians must face up to the serious but pressing challenges. We *should* be concerned and take more than a passing interest in the material world, for at least four reasons. First, we owe it to ourselves. We have to live in the world, it is the only home we have! Second, we owe it to our children and their children. We must pass on a usable world to those who follow us. It is, after all, their rightful inheritance and we have only borrowed it from them. Third, we owe it to the Church not to waste the chance of showing that the Gospel is relevant and about the whole world, not just about people's souls. Fourth, and most important, we owe it to God. This is God's world not ours to do with as we please. It is, after all, his creation that is at stake.

Ultimately, Christians must reclaim the spiritual territory now occupied by "the greens" which is becoming a confused and confusing battleground of competing ideologies, philosophies and beliefs.

Christian/green convergence

Yet it would be wrong to assume that there is an unbridgeable gulf between Christianity and the green movement, because there are signs of an emerging convergence between the two. This is unlikely ever to be a complete synthesis. Indeed, there is no reason why it should be. But at least the two sides are starting to explore common ground, and to challenge and inspire each other.

Two decades ago, at the start of the first wave of recent environmental concern, American Lutheran pastor Kenneth Alpers noted that "ecology has become more than a hitherto rather obscure branch of biology; it has become a hot political issue, and a possible new symbol of the generation gap. It may become a fruitful new model for 'doing' Christian theology and ethics."[2] But, interestingly, he envisaged such a model emerging from the green camp rather than the Christian one. In his view, "the development of an adequate theological response to current environmental issues will be found not by beginning with deductions from Christian sources and dogmas, but by first looking at the complex nature of the environment itself. Unless we are listening, we will not be heard."[3] Others have since echoed the view that Christianity is more likely to be influenced by green thinking, than *vice versa*.[4]

But this emerging convergence is not without problems for Christianity. The most serious relate to the bundle of religious ideas associated with the green movement which are not compatible with Christianity – such as pantheism, the New Age movement, and even environmental concern as idolatry in its own right. There is the additional problem that some greens use inferred attitudes towards the environment as a means of discrediting Christian teaching, traditions and faith.

Problems also arise from the fact that most of the calls for Christianity to become more green have been coming from greens rather than from Christians. The impetus has come from without not within. This might be inevitable, but it means that Christians might have to react in ways they would not otherwise feel comfortable with. It also means that Christianity is failing to occupy and hold on to the moral high ground in the green debate.

One illustration of this external pressure comes from feminist green writer Charlene Spretnak who suggests that Christianity and Judaism "should stop being ashamed of their 'pagan' inheritance, *which is substantial*, and should proudly proclaim their many inherent ties to Nature".[5]

But it is simply not true that Christians have not been trying to get their own house in order and have sat back and waited for the greens to bring the debate to them. One tangible reflection of Christian involvement is the emergence of the stewardship movement within the broader context of Christian lifestyles.

LIFESTYLE: WEALTH AND POSSESSIONS

In the last chapter we explored the basis of stewardship as a gift of God, and as something we are all responsible for. We looked at stewardship there in the specific context of nature and natural resources, but of course we are called to be stewards of all of God's material gifts.

Guidelines

While the Bible does not tell us specifically whether we should buy a bigger car, have no car or keep the one we have, it does give us certain principles by which we must measure our lifestyle and thus our success at being God's stewards.[6] Such principles or guidelines are more important now than ever before, in an age of materialism and consumerism which teaches us that success is found in what we possess and that happiness depends on money.[7]

Although the Bible is not a resource management handbook, it does contain more than a few clues about how we should treat the material gifts that God so freely gives to us. This includes the gift of wealth and possessions, as well as natural raw materials (like energy, water, earth and fertile soil). The following guidelines[8] seem particularly relevant -

1. We are stewards not owners of our possessions
Like nature, our possessions and wealth belong to God not us. Thus we are stewards not owners of our wealth, which is part of the material gifts of creation. But although our wealth and possessions are not ultimately our own private property, we are still empowered and encouraged by God to use them. The New Testament steward was responsible for all aspects of the management of the estate (including its material production and the people on it), even though the estate was not his.

2. Our possessions are a blessing from God
Material wellbeing and even prosperity are blessings from God. Provided we recognize that our wealth and possessions are a gift from God, and we use them as God intended, we have no reason to feel compromised if we seem to be well endowed, Scripture confirms. Poverty is not idealized, and suffering, hunger, or exploitation are not biblical virtues. Neither is prosperity condemned as evil in itself. It is not ownership that matters, but how we acquired the wealth and possessions, how we value them, and what we do with them.

In his covenant dealings with people God rewards obedience with material prosperity, but he always retains sole ownership of everything. For example, Abraham became wealthy as part of God's promise to him, and the people of Israel moved into a land flowing with milk and honey. Jesus promised that those who first seek the kingdom of God will have all things added to them. So

God does not condemn us simply because we are wealthy. Some of God's best servants (like Abraham) were wealthy. But they didn't hoard their wealth or regard it as the most important thing in their lives.

3. Material success is not a guarantee of righteousness
Some people argue that if material prosperity is a blessing from God, surely those who are wealthy and successful must be righteous because they have been blessed by God. But this isn't the case. To use material prosperity as a measure of God's faithfulness to a person or people is to misunderstand the nature of his blessing. Not all wealth or all possessions are gained by fair or righteous means. In some cases wealth might derive from oppression and exploitation, which God regards as sins. There is obviously no way that God will condone wealth won in a bank robbery, won by corruption, or won by selling the products of slave-labour.

So although the Old Testament says that God gives prosperity to the righteous (for example, in Psalm 37:3-4), it denies the opposite – that wealth and prosperity always indicate righteousness. There is also a constant tension between the promise of prosperity for the righteous, and the simple fact that the righteous are sometimes poor and needy through no fault of their own. This ambivalence surrounding prosperity and its interpretation poses particular problems for Christians.

4. Possessions are to be enjoyed but kept in perspective
The Bible does not teach that we should be self-conscious about our possessions, provided that we have the right attitude towards them. Whilst Jesus was a man of few possessions, he was not an ascetic and found little comfort in overt self-denial. He glorified neither poverty nor

abstention from pleasure, and his attitude was that good things like food were there to be enjoyed. But they were not essential for him, and he was not attached to them (see, for example, Matthew 6:25–34).

The apostle Paul, like Jesus, had no attachment to material comforts and was happy to enjoy good things but not to get hooked on them. We see this, for example, in the free and open way in which Paul shared whatever he had and in his contentment in all circumstances (Philippians 4:11).

5. Obsession with possessions is unhealthy and unbiblical

We often forget that the principal source of our human dignity is the fact that God created us in his image. It is easy to fall into the trap of believing that dignity comes with wealth, status or power. Hence an obsession with wealth and possessions is not uncommon. Yet they can become idols for us to worship, and we can readily let them come between us and God. Paul pointed out that "we brought nothing into the world, and we can take nothing out of it" and "people who want to get rich fall into temptation and a trap and into many foolish and harmful desires that plunge men into ruin and destruction. For the love of money is a root of all kinds of evil. Some people, eager for money, have wandered from the faith" (1 Timothy 6:7–10).

Jesus warned those who direct their attention and affection on money that, as a result, they have less of both for God. He stressed that "where your treasure is, there your heart will be also. . . . No-one can serve two masters. Either he will hate the one and love the other, or he will be devoted to the one and despise the other. You cannot serve both God and Money." (Matthew 6:21–4).

Jesus also warned against being so obsessed with our wealth that we keep it to ourselves. He told the story (Luke 12:13–21) of the rich young fool who believed that all he had to do was store up more and more crops and possessions then he could "take life easy; eat, drink and be merry" (verse 19).

Clearly it is not biblical to accumulate wealth and material possessions simply for the sake of it, because we can start to crave for them out of sheer greed. It is also unbiblical to gain wealth by injustice and oppression. The real question about money for each of us is not how much (or little) we have, but what role it plays in our life.

6. God requires total commitment and trust

God provides for all our needs by controlling nature. He also provides all the material things we need (but not necessarily all that we *want*). In return, he expects us to be totally committed to him and his kingdom. Jesus illustrates this by the story of the man who found treasure hidden in a field then sold all he possessed to buy that field; and the merchant with the fine pearls (Matthew 13:44–6).

God also expects us to trust him, not only for the major decisions in life but also the small ones. Jesus said that commitment requires total trust, so that we should leave material things such as food and clothing to God and trust that he will provide what we need (Matthew 7:7–12).

Jesus speaks of these things in the story of the rich young man (Mark 10:17–31). When he asked Jesus how could he inherit eternal life, he was told "Go, sell everything you have and give to the poor, and you will have treasure in heaven. Then come, follow me" (verse 21).

The young man in question was wealthy and sad at the prospect of having to give it all up. Wealth is one of the greatest barriers between man and God.

7. *We are expected to share our resources with others*
We have already noted that it is what we do with our money and possessions that counts, not how much we have. The Bible suggests that one of the best uses of our material resources is to assist those less fortunate than ourselves. For instance, Psalm 41:1 tells us to use our money to help the poor, and Paul stressed the importance of those with money passing at least some of it on to those without (2 Corinthians 8:14). We are instructed to give cheerfully (2 Corinthians 9:7), not reluctantly.

God's special concern is for the poor and the needy, who are often poor and needy because of unjust distribution of the available resources. They should have first call on any resources which are made available (Luke 6:20–1).

A genuine concern for others (koinonia), exhibited for example in the communal sharing of possessions and meals, was a hallmark of the early Christian church (Acts 2:43–7, 4:32–5, 5:11). The sharing did not necessarily mean a total rejection of private ownership. It was more that people were released from the *need* for private possession (Acts 4:32). This was a gradual process which took place according to the needs of the community. It flowed from the deep spirituality, love and trust which bound the early Church together; it was not a hard and fast rule to be obeyed at all times and at all costs.[9]

The Christian "good life"
The biblical lifestyle which centres on Jesus should be different from the prevailing values and lifestyle of con-

temporary culture.[10] It should not centre on wealth or material possessions, it should naturally include sharing with and caring for other people, and it should be based on moderation. The Christian lifestyle should emphasize quality of existence and reverence for life.[11]

But it should also be a life of celebration, not a sense of constraint or imposed limits reluctantly adopted. Within these sorts of guidelines, we should work and pay attention to what is useful, but we should also enjoy life.[12] This might require us to re-order our lives to make room for celebration, delight, worship and contemplation.

Such qualities should find favour amongst green thinkers because they are entirely compatible with the green idea of "the good life".[13] The green "good life" seeks to reduce ambition and desires and avoid competition between people by embracing voluntary simplicity and love and respect for all things. It is based on shedding what is unnecessary and seeking simplicity and frugality.

SOLUTIONS

Christianity and conservation have different views on what we should do about the environmental crisis. The secular view is that the crisis – a *practical* problem – requires a *practical* solution involving science, politics, changes in behaviour, consumer patterns and so on. To Christians the crisis – a *spiritual* problem – requires a *spiritual* solution involving a change in individual people who must repent of their self-centred ways and be reconciled to God through a faith in Jesus.

In reality, both are required. We need to adopt both spiritual and practical measures if we are to do anything significant about the environmental crisis. There are no simple solutions, and different dimensions of the crisis will ultimately have to be tackled differently.

Christians face at least three major challenges if they are to get their own environmental house in order.[14] The first is to develop a fully biblical approach to creation (along the lines we considered in the last chapter). The second challenge is to accept that our lifestyles must change, sometimes in ways which are costly, if we are truly to care for the earth. Challenge three is to do something, rather than nothing, perhaps by joining groups and organizations committed to change.

SPIRITUAL ISSUES

Major environmental problems like global warming, sea level rise and loss of species are here and they are serious. Secular conservation offers a rather hopeless outlook, because such complex problems are going to be hard to solve. Indeed, for many of the key problems no realistic solution is in sight. But Christianity offers hope, through the promised redemption of all creation.

Many Christians see a real solution in world mission and evangelism, presenting the Gospel of salvation to all people around the world. Then they can make up their own minds whether or not to believe in and follow Jesus. Put bluntly, the sooner everyone has a chance to hear and respond to the Gospel, the quicker mankind will put itself right again with God and the sooner Jesus returns, the quicker nature will be redeemed. Eight centuries ago St Francis of Assisi took Jesus's command to "go into all the world and preach the good news to all creation" (Mark 16:15) so seriously and literally that he even preached to the birds and wolves!

There is general agreement between greens and Christians that we hold the key to solving the environmental problems, although Christians may be excused a little in thinking that God should intervene and sort out the mess. If, as we know from experience, God is both transcendent and immanent, why does he not step in and simply make the world a better place for us all? He did, after all, create everything (including us) so repairing the damage must be well within his means. This is basically the same question as "Why does God allow disasters to happen, and suffering to occur?"

The simple but truthful answer, of course, is that we just don't know. We can't read God's mind, and we can't see things as he does. Some would say that God uses things like suffering, disasters and environmental problems to teach us lessons (echoing the Old Testament view that God uses nature as a reward or punishment). But God loves the world and everything in it, and an alternative interpretation is that God wants us to surrender our lives to him unconditionally. He could act on our behalf (he did with the Flood, after all) but he wants us to make the first step, towards him. He gave us free will and expects us to use it. This has clear implications for each of us as individuals, but it also underlines the responsibility of all Christians to engage in sharing the good news of the Gospel of Jesus with the people all around them.

Individual responsibilities

There are a number of other spiritual things we should each be doing as individuals, as well.

First, we should get right with God. Jesus said "Do not set your heart on what you will eat or drink; do not worry about it. For the pagan world runs after all such things, and your Father knows that you need them. But seek his kingdom, and these things will be given to you as well" (Luke 12:29–31).

Second, we should use the Christian's most powerful tool, prayer. Pray for wisdom in how you should lead your life, what quantity and type of things you buy and use, what you do with things you no longer require. Pray for damaging activities to stop, for environmental damage to heal or be repaired, and for everyone (including other Christians) to take a more caring attitude to the world about us. Prayer and regular communion with God are without doubt the most important contributions the Christian can make to the environmental crisis.

Third, we should regularly read God's word in the Bible. The Bible is not an environmental text-book, but it does contain a great deal of relevant guidance and there are a good many lessons to be learnt from Old Testament characters, Jesus and people in the early Church. We should search the Scriptures regularly, and let them shape what we do, how we do it, and why we do it.

Fourth, we should check our motives. We should ask ourselves why we are interested in the state of the environment. Are we genuinely concerned, and committed to doing something about it, or are we merely jumping on the green bandwagon?

Fifth, we should recognize that the whole green debate is a spiritual minefield, and enter it with our eyes open. Paul warns against falling prey to false "philosophy and empty deceit" (Colossians 2:8), and advises us to "seek the things that are above, where Christ is" (Colossians 3:1).

Sixth, we should try to get our priorities right. This might start with respecting the earth as God's creation, accepting God's concern and wisdom, acknowledging that Jesus is Lord. We might also repent and ask God to forgive both us and others for attitudes, values, habits and practices which damage the environment. We should also seek God's guidance on how we should treat the world around us – through prayer, from reading the Bible, and from learning from other people and situations.

PRACTICAL ISSUES – LIFESTYLE

As well as taking these spiritual matters seriously, we need to ask ourselves "What can we do in practical terms to help solve the environmental crisis"? The easy option is to sit back and ignore the problem, or convince ourselves that the problem is too big for us individually to do anything significant. But there *are* things we can do. Each individual thing may be small, but if everyone made some simple changes in their daily routines the cumulative impact could be large.

Here is not the place to look in detail at how we should use our car, clean our house or look after our garden in ways which are environment-friendly. There are plenty of books which offer advice on such things, such as the best-selling *Green Consumer Guide* by John Elkington and Julia Hailes (1988). But we can think about some of the general issues, using how we shop and what we do with our rubbish as examples.

General guidelines

Our lifestyle should flow out of our spirituality. It should be the practical outworking of a genuine commitment to Christ, rooted in a respect for God's created world. As such the Christian lifestyle should be one of celebration (of God's love and provision) and thus joy, based on restraint in what we do and taking care of our needs not our greed.

We should also be aware of how our way of living affects other people, because often we benefit from the suffering of others. For example we might exploit other people as a source of cheap labour, we might damage their environment by buying products from it or we may pollute them with our wastes.

We should also remember that everything we do affects the environment somewhere, somehow, some time. When you turn on the tap at home, for example, think where that water is coming from, and at what cost to the environment. Think where the waste water goes to, what chemicals it might contain (cleaning chemicals, for example, which you may have put in it) and what ecological damage it might do as it flows downstream and out to sea.

Green shopping

Most of us have call to shop, and to suggest never buying anything, or only working off some primitive bartering and exchange system, is unrealistic. So the question is *how* we should shop, not *whether* we should.

Wise shopping (in terms of what we buy, and how much we buy) is the objective. First, we should stop and think carefully about whether we really do need new things or whether we just want them. For staple items, like food, the answer is normally obvious. But for luxury items we have more choice. Are we buying just to keep up with the mythical Joneses, for the street credibility of wearing this year's colours or the status of being seen with possessions of a certain style?

Having decided that we do need to buy certain things, we should set about the task mindful of the fact that we can use the economic power of our weekly shop to change the world.[15] Some companies aim to provide equal opportunities for women and minority groups, for example, whereas others don't. We can have an effect on some environmental problems if we buy from companies which do not use animal testing for consumer products (foods, drugs, cosmetics and cleaners), and from companies which use environment-friendly technologies and manufacturing processes.

If we are genuine about trying to lead a green lifestyle, we should think seriously about trying to identify and then avoid products[16] which –

- are likely to endanger the health of the consumer or others,
- cause significant damage to environment during manufacture, use or disposal,
- consume a disproportionate amount of energy during manufacture, use or disposal,
- cause unnecessary waste (through over-packing or unduly short useful life),
- use materials derived from threatened species or from threatened environments,
- involve unnecessary use of, or cruelty to, animals (in toxicity testing, for example).

There is no doubt that consumer power is real, and that informed consumers can make a real difference to the world. Public pressure for environmentally-friendly products has been mounting in recent years, and the marketplace is starting to respond. For example, harmful CFCs are now being removed from most aerosol cans and foam plastics, and biodegradeable forms of packaging are being developed and used.

We can't necessarily buy a clean environment, but by

buying environment-friendly products we can cut down the amount of damage we are inflicting on the planet. Sensible shoppers are friends of the earth.

Recycling and disposal

Waste disposal creates some difficult environmental problems, and it is not confined to toxic wastes from factories. Even domestic wastes, the things we would normally simply put out for the dustbin man to take away, need to be disposed of properly. Landfill sites (where most domestic waste normally ends up) are not limitless, either in size or number, and dumping often leads to contamination of local water supplies as well as unsightly tips and wind-blow of rubbish over the surrounding area.

We can make a significant contribution to the problems by producing less waste at home. The easiest option is to buy less (hence have less to dispose of ultimately), and make sure that what we do buy is durable and not over-packaged. We can also give away things we have spare to other people who could make use of them, helping the environment and those in need at the same time.

Organic wastes (like food) can be disposed of on the garden compost heap, and eventually put back in the soil. The rest of our wastes should be disposed of thoughtfully. Special guidance is needed when disposing of hazardous wastes, like old fridges (which contain CFC coolants); they should not be simply dumped.

Items which can be recycled, like newspapers and glass bottles, should be taken to local collection points for recycling. There is at least one church-based recycling company in Britain, the Community Recycling Opportunities Programme (CROP) in Milton Keynes run by

Baptist minister Robert Brown. He sees this as "exercising a ministry to recycle people, a community and myself – as I try to take a lead in expressing the down-to-earth love for [God's] creation . . . [and] helping people to love God's world in a practical way".[17]

PRACTICAL ISSUES – ACTIVISM

A third way in which we can play a part is by becoming involved in environmental affairs. This might involve a purely passive role, like joining groups such as local nature conservation trusts or the National Trust, or more green groups such as Greenpeace or Friends of the Earth. The annual subscription to such groups is used to support their environmental programme and in return the member receives regular information, magazines and merchandising catalogues.

At the other end of the spectrum, it might involve playing an active role in environmental campaigning. Extreme examples would include the antics of Animal Liberation groups, and the media-grabbing initiatives of Greenpeace activists (whose exploits include disturbing dumping of nuclear waste at sea, using rubber dinghies). Less extreme active involvement might include organizing local litter-collecting and similar environmental improvement events, and taking part in peaceful demonstrations about environmental issues.

In the middle of the spectrum are activities like letter writing to companies and government ministers. Green shopping is also a form of environmental activism! So also is using one's natural talents and gifts in the service of raising people's awareness about environmental problems – for example through writing, drama, photographic and artistic exhibitions.

Environmental activism raises some thorny problems, because whilst some forms are good and quite scriptural (through practical involvement to help others), some are clearly not. To what extent is it justifiable to break the law or infringe the rights of other people when registering a point, for example?

We would do well to remember that Christians part company with secular greens in a number of ways, too. For example, Christians could not accept the common green view that people and animals are equal and trees and animals have rights. Christians should also be on the lookout for signs of infiltration of environmental groups by the New Age movement, although these are often very difficult to detect. Equally, many environmental activities either reflect or are directly based on a belief in nature mysticism (as reflected, for example, in solar cycles and earth rhythms), so there are attendant dangers of earth worship, either explicitly or implicitly.

CHRISTIAN INITIATIVES

The Christian Church is in something of an ambivalent position as regards playing an active role within the green debate. On the one hand, there is no doubt that we are all called to be stewards of God's creation. It is also true that the Church has sometimes led the field in enlightened use of resources. Think of the effective and sustainable management of extensive monastic estates by the Benedictines and Cistercians, for example.

But more times than not Christians have failed to

accept the calling to stewardship or to take a lead in the environmental debate.

Failure

There are a number of reasons why Christians and the Church have not taken a lead in environmental affairs. History shows that many missionary activities overseas, in the name of the Church, exploited and oppressed indigenous peoples. But the record also shows that they radically altered environments, often by importing and adopting European land management practices which were patently unsuited to the territories in question. The sad tale of Puritan farming in New England tells a similar story.

Today's Church generally shows remarkably little interest in managing church lands (which in some instances are vast and highly productive) in ecological ways. Few churchyards, which often offer variety of habitat within heavily built-up areas, are maintained in ways which benefit wildlife. This could be something as simple as leaving some areas of grass or hedge uncut. Beyond the territorial boundary of the church, there are still relatively few signs of widespread church involvement in conservation and sustainable resource-management schemes.

Promise

But it is not all bad news. Although Christians (individually and collectively) have doubtless missed many golden opportunities through the ages to put into practice the divine commission to be stewards of God's creation, they have not abandoned the field altogether and have made some moves in the right direction.

One important development has been the growing

number of contributions to the development of a green theology. A 1971 review of what had been written about the links between Christianity and ecology had relatively few books and articles to consider, and most of those had been written by ecologists.[18] The task would be much easier today, since a number of important books on the subject have appeared. A particularly interesting book, written from an evangelical perspective by members of the Calvin Center for Christian Scholarship in the USA, is *Earthkeeping; Christian stewardship of natural resources*.[19]

A number of green theology books have been published recently. One classic is *God in creation* by Jurgen Moltmann[20] who sees the environmental crisis as so urgent that we are witnessing "the beginning of a life and death struggle for creation on the earth". Sean McDonagh, an Irish Columban missionary, builds on the theme of unity in creation in *To care for the earth; a call to a new theology*[21] and, more recently, in *The greening of the church*.[22] Similar ground is explored by Church of Scotland minister Ian Bradley in *God is Green*[23] (1990) and by Christian Tim Cooper, a prominent member of the British Green Party, in *Green Christianity*.[24]

As well as the growing green Christian literature, there is no shortage of guidance on green-type matters from different branches of the Christian church. Green-oriented Catholics have the papal encyclicals[25] to turn to – especially Pope Pius XI's 1931 encyclical *Quadragesimo anno (Forty Years After)*. This established three cardinal principles relevant to environment and lifestyle. The first was personalism, meaning that the goal of society is to develop and enrich the individual human person. The second was subsidiarity, meaning that no organization should be bigger than necessary and nothing should be done by a larger and higher social unit than can be done effectively by a lower and smaller unit. The third principal was pluralism, meaning that a healthy society is characterized by a wide variety of intermediate groups freely flourishing between the individual and the state.

Other Christian groups have published statements aimed at guiding thinking and action within the environmental field.[26] The Catholic Bishops of Appalachia issued a statement titled *This land is my home; a pastoral letter on powerlessness in Appalachia*, which calls for worker-owned businesses and community-based economics. Similar ideas are embodied in *Strangers and guests; toward community in the heartland*, issued by the Catholic bishops of the heartland (Midwest USA), and in the American Lutheran Church's *The land; God's giving, our caring*. The last two look particularly at ecological use of the land. For instance, the heartland Bishops propose such principles as "the land should be distributed equitably" and "the land's workers should be able to become the land's owners", and favour the taxing of agricultural land according to its productive value rather than its speculative value.

Environmental matters have also appeared on the agenda of the Church of England General Synod's Board of Social Responsibility, which published the 1980 report *Our responsibility for the living environment*. The World Council of Churches project on Justice, Peace and the Integrity of Creation promises to yield valuable fruits in terms of a better awareness of the links between behaviour, poverty and environment.

A Christian presence in the environmental field is also evident in other ways. Many of the international Christian relief, aid and development agencies (like Tear Fund and Cafod) place a great emphasis on ecological factors in their projects, thus both caring for the poor and conserving the earth at the same time. A fair proportion of the resources of such agencies is invested in education and training programmes which are designed to teach and encourage people in developing countries to adopt land and resource management practices which are sustainable and environment-friendly.

Another hopeful sign is the work of the international network of religion and conservation groups established and co-ordinated by the World-wide Fund for Nature (WWF). The network was established following a conference in Assisi in Italy in September 1986, with the belief that "the major religions have the opportunity, and indeed the duty, to provide their members with a clear philosophy about man's responsibility towards the natural world." In addition to establishing a world-wide network of interested people and organizations, the network publishes a glossy quarterly journal (*The New Road*) and has organized a series of major inter-faith gatherings and celebrations around the world.

In Britain a bridge between Christians and greens has been provided by a group called Christian Ecology Link, formed in 1981 (originally as Christian Ecology Group) to spread ecological insights among Christian people and churches and to spread Christian insights into the green movement. It is supported by Christians from most traditions, including Anglican, Orthodox, Roman Catholic, House Churches and Free Churches, including Quakers. The group seeks to stimulate interest, discussion, new awareness and practical action by means of a newsletter, conferences and occasional publications.

A growing number of individual Christians and Christian groups are starting to take seriously their role as stewards of God's creation, and they are doing this in a variety of ways. It is no longer true to say that Christians are not playing a part in seeking solutions for the environmental crisis. But we cannot be complacent because there is plenty of scope for more Christians to become involved, for those who are involved to increase and diversify their involvement, and for the overall axis of Christian involvement in the green debate to become more mainstream.

The challenge for Christians

Our fundamental responsibility to act as stewards of God's creation means that Christians have a duty to take part in rather than exclude themselves from the debate. But in doing that we should be careful to retain what it is about and within our faith that makes us Christians, not just concerned individuals. We need, for example, to take seriously our spiritual responsibilities (prayer, Bible study, sharing with others, and so on) and give them top priority. Similarly, we must not waste the opportunities which the green debate presents for us to speak of Christian stewardship and through that to share the Gospel of Jesus and the good news of the Bible with others. Equally, we should be prepared to defend the record of Christianity when non-believers repeat the well-worn (indeed, by now almost threadbare) argument that the Judeo-Christian tradition is the root of the environmental crisis.

For the benefit of the earth, to put the record straight and to capitalize on the opportunity to witness for Jesus we should welcome the emergence of a green Christianity. More than that, we should be turning green ourselves!

NOTES

Chapter One

1. Quoted from Montefiore (1970).
2. The word "green" was first used in this ecological sense as recently as 1978 (Button 1988).
3. Paehlke (1989).
4. Paehlke (1989).
5. Christian Sociologist and writer David Lyon (1989 p. 7) describes Jonathan Porritt as "a man of huge vision and a deep understanding of green issues" who "never loses sight of the wood for the trees".
6. Quoted from Porritt and Winner (1988).
7. Porritt (1984).
8. Pepper (1987).
9. The examples quote data from *World Resources* 1988.
10. Keating (1989 p. 45).
11. Park (1986 p. 7).
12. Park (1981 p. 118).
13. Quoted in Park (1987 p. 115).
14. Quoted from Tuan (1974, p. 216).
15. Meadows *et al* (1972).
16. Figures quoted by Greig, Pike and Selby (1987).
17. Quoted from World Comission on Environment and Development (1987).

Chapter Two

1. A good starting point is *The green consumer guide* by John Elkington and Julia Hailes (1988).
2. Schwarz (1974 p. 326) coined the term "pleonexia" to describe this obsession with accumulating goods and material possessions.
3. Martin (1970).
4. Quoted in *WWF News* January 1989, p. 10.
5. Keller (1971).

6. Quoted in Fritsch (1980 p. 291).
7. Meyer-Abich (1988).

8. Carpenter (1987).
9. Button (1988 p. 22).

Chapter Three

1. Based on a suggestion by Walter (1982).
2. *Collins English Dictionary* (1979).
3. Eckbo (1987).
4. Berry (1975).
5. Dietrich (1980).
6. John Walter (1982).
7. Skolimowski (1973, p. 50).
8. Morris (1981).
9. Skolimowski (1975).
10. Walter (1982).
11. Dietrich (1980 p. 4).
12. White (1962).
13. Skolimowski (1973 p. 51).
14. Skolimowski (1973 p. 51).
15. Skolimowski hails Bacon as "the most articulate spokesman for the new science, although alas not its most successful practitioner" (Skolimowski 1973 p. 52).
16. Quoted in Skolimowski (1973 p. 52).
17. Quoted in Skolimowski (1975 p. 13).
18. Skolimowski (1973 p. 52).
19. Dietrich (1980).
20. Dietrich (1980 p. 6).
21. Walter (1982).
22. Dietrich (1980).
23. Term coined by Skolimowski (1975, p. 10).
24. Skolimowski (1975 p. 12) points out that utilitarianism was soon vulgarized to mean "the biggest number of material goods to the largest possible number of people".
25. Biggins (1978 p. 220).
26. Roszak (1972).
27. Allen (1974, p. 317).
28. *Collins English Dictionary* (1979).
29. Walter (1982).
30. Morris (1981).
31. Roszak favours ecology as an integrating perspective because "it is the one science that seems capable of assimilating moral principles and visionary experience" (Roszak 1972).
32. Foley (1988).
33. Foley (1988).
34. Naess (1988).
35. Paehlke (1989).

Chapter Four

1. Quote from Icke (1990 p. 198).
2. Catherine von Ruhland (1989) points out that "the anti-materialism inherent in Green philosophy attracts all kinds of spiritually-inclined people".
3. Dasmann (1974).
4. Alpers noted that "the younger self-styled 'eco-freaks' usually prefer Zen or Tao" (Alpers 1971 p. 308).
5. Spretnak (1986 p. 52).
6. Icke (1990 p. 201).
7. Omo-Fadaka (1974).
8. Baird Callicott (1982).
9. Jacobs (1978 p. 5–6).
10. Callicott (1982 p. 310).
11. Quoted by Royston (1979 p. 1).
12. Sylvan and Bennett (1988 p. 148).
13. Sylvan and Bennett (1988 p. 152).
14. Barash (1973).
15. de Silva (1978).
16. de Silva (1978 p. 9).
17. Ophuls (1977).
18. Schumacher (1973).
19. Ophuls (1977).
20. Kumar (1974).
21. *The Times* 18 September 1989.
22. Lovelock (1987).
23. Myers (1985, 1990).
24. Goldsmith (1988 p. 169).
25. Goldsmith links Gaia with Taoism and Buddhism, and suggests that all men should follow The Way (of Taoism) "if they are to have lives compatible with Gaian order and hence if they are to maximize their welfare" (1988 p. 179).
26. Stott (1989).
27. Berry (1988 p. 4).
28. Higton (1989).
29. Berry (1988 p. 6).
30. Runcie (1989).
31. Stott (1989).

Chapter Five

1. White (1967 p. 1206).
2. White (1967 p. 1205).
3. White (1967 p. 1205).
4. White (1967 p. 1207).
5. For example, Cox (1965) argued that the creation account in Genesis distinguished man from nature, and nature from God; this biblically-based "disenchantment" with nature made it "available

for man's use" (p. 23) and encouraged the development of science and technology.

6. Derr (1975 p. 40).
7. Quoted from Derr (1975 p. 39).
8. Derr (1975 p. 45).
9. Tuan (1970 p. 247).
10. Kay (1985).
11. Kay (1985).
12. Doughty (1981) and Livingstone (1983).
13. Tuan (1970).

14. Dubos (1973 p. 56).
15. Tuan (1970).
16. Derr (1975 p. 43).
17. Tuan (1970 p. 247).
18. Santmire (1975) and Moncrief (1970).
19. Wrightsman (1970).
20. Hiers (1984 p. 43) and Wrightsman (1970).
21. Hiers (1984).
22. Button (1988 p. 234).
23. Derr (1975 p. 43).
24. Botkin and Keller (1987).
25. Wright (1970 p. 852).

Chapter Six

1. Echlin (1989).
2. Santmire (1980).
3. Quoted from White (1947 p. 432).
4. Echlin (1989 p. 10).
5. Dubos (1973 p. 56).
6. White (1947).
7. White (1947 p. 433).
8. Dubos (1973).
9. McKee (1974).
10. Quoted from Dubos (1973 p. 60).

11. McKee (1974).
12. Simmons (1988).
13. Jacobs (1978 p. 9).
14. Kay (1985 p. 131).
15. Jacobs (1978).
16. Kay and Brown (1985 p. 263).
17. Kay and Brown (1985).
18. Flores (1983).
19. Flores (1983).

Chapter Seven

1. Hiers (1984).
2. Bratton (1984).
3. Hiers (1984).
4. Ehrenfeld and Bentley (1985).
5. Santmire (1975).
6. Wright (1970 p. 851).
7. Bird (1981).

8. Innes (1987).
9. Fackre (1971 p. 214).
10. Ehrenfeld and Bentley (1985).
11. Kay (1988 p. 315).
12. Ehrenfeld and Bentley (1985).
13. Bird (1981 p. 154).

14. Innes (1987).
15. Pollard (1984 p. 132).
16. Pelcovitz (1970 p. 29).
17. Berry (1979 p. 20).
18. Berry (1979 p. 21).
19. Ehrenfeld and Bentley (1985).
20. Ehrenfeld and Bentley (1985 p. 306).
21. Helfand (1971).
22. Gordis (1970 p. 8).
23. Gaebelein (1980 p. 35).

24. Ehrenfeld and Bentley (1985 p. 310).
25. Blidstein (1966 p. 48).
26. Gordis (1970 p. 8).
27. Collison (1986).
28. Fackre (1971).
29. Pelcovitz (1970 p. 24–25).
30. Fackre (1971).
31. Caldecott (1986 p. 5).
32. Berry (1975).
33. Barr (1972).

Chapter Eight

1. Baer (1977 p. 488).
2. Alpers (1971 p. 293).
3. Alpers (1971 p. 308).
4. Schwarz (1990).
5. Spretnak (1986 p. 53).
6. Gaebelein (1980).
7. Branon (1990).
8. West (1975), Davids (1980) and Gaebelein (1980).
9. Davids (1980).
10. Davids (1980).
11. Elder (1970).
12. Baer (1977).
13. Sylvan and Bennett (1988).

14. Lyon (1989 p. 8).
15. Council on Economic Priorities (1989).
16. 21 CC, September 1989, p. 47.
17. Brown (1990).
18. Alpers (1971).
19. Wilkinson (1980).
20. Moltmann (1985).
21. McDonagh (1986).
22. McDonagh (1990).
23. Bradley (1990).
24. Cooper (1990).
25. Spretnak (1985 p. 67).
26. Spretnak (1985 p. 65).

REFERENCES

Allen, R. (1974) Hunting peoples; harmony between community and environment. *Resurgence* 5; 3–5.

Alpers, K. P. (1971) Starting points for an ecological theology; a bibliographical survey. 292–312 in M. E. Marty & D. G. Peerman (eds) *New Theology* No 8. New York, Macmillan.

Attfield, R. (1983) Christian attitudes to nature. *Journal of the History of Ideas* 44; 369–86.

Baer, R. A. (1977) Higher education, the church and environmental values. *Natural Resources Journal* 3; 477–91.

Barash, D. P. (1973) The ecologist as Zen master. *American Midland Naturalist* 89; 214–17.

Barbour, I. G. (1975) Science, religion and the counter-culture. *Zygon* 10; 380–97.

Barr, J. (1972) Man and nature – the ecological controversy and the Old Testament. *Bulletin of the John Rylands Library* 55; 9–32.

Berry, H. (1988) *New Age Movement.* Lincoln Nebraska, Back to the Bible.

Berry, S. (1975) *Ecology and ethics.* Leicester, Inter-Varsity Press.

Berry, W. (1979) The gift of good land. *Sierra Club Bulletin* 64; 20–6.

Biggins, D. R. (1978) The social context of ecology. *Ecologist Quarterly* Autumn; 218–26.

Bird, P. A. (1981) Male and female he created them; Genesis 1:27b in the context of the priestly act of creation. *Harvard Theological Review* 74; 129–59.

Blachford, K. (1979) Morals and values in geographic education; toward a metaphysics of the environment. *Geographical Education* 3: 423–57.

Black, J. (1970) *The dominion of man; the search for ecological responsibility*. Edinburgh, Edinburgh University Press.

Blidstein, G. J. (1966) Man and nature in the Sabbatical Year. *Tradition* IX (4); 48–55.

Botkin, D. B. and E. A. Keller (1987) *Environmental Studies; earth as a living planet*. Columbus Ohio, Merrill.

Bradley, I. (1990) *God is green*. London, Darton Longman and Todd.

Branon, D. (1990) For the love of money. *Discovery Digest* 10–17.

Bratton, S. P. (1984) Christian ecotheology and the Old Testament. *Environmental Ethics* 6; 195–209.

Brown, R. (1988) Resources and religion. *The New Road* 5; 7.

Brown, R. (1990) A down-to-earth love. *Church of England Newspaper* 26 January; 6.

Button, P. H. (1988) *A dictionary of green ideas*. London, Routledge.

Caldecott, S. (1986) A Christian cosmology. *Resurgence* 115; 5–6.

Callicott, J. B. (1982) Traditional American Indian and Western European attitudes toward nature; an overview. *Environmental Ethics* 4; 293–318.

Carpenter, R. A. (1987) What to do while waiting for an environmental ethic. *The Environmental Professional* 9; 327–35.

Collison, J. G. F. (1986) Biblical perspectives on stewardship of earth's resources. *Bangalore Theological Forum* 18; 153–60.

Cooper, T. (1990) *Green Christianity*. London, Hodder & Stoughton.

Council on Economic Priorities (1989) *Shopping for a better world; America at the checkout*. Newcastle upon Tyne, Council on Economic Priorities and New Consumer.

Cox, H. (1965) *The Secular City*. New York, Macmillan.

Crowther-Green, M. (1985) *The steward; a biblical symbol for today*. Oxford, Diocesan Church House.

Dasmann, R. F. (1974) Conservation, counter-culture and separate realities. *Environmental Conservation* 1; 133–7.

Davids, P. H. (1980) New Testament foundations for living more simply. 40–58 in R. J. Sider (ed) *Living more simply; Biblical principles and practical models*. London, Hodder and Stoughton.

Derr, T. S. (1975) Religion's responsibility for the ecological crisis; an argument run amok. *Worldview* 18; 39–45.

Dietrich, D. J. (1980) Christianity and conservation; an alternative to environmental exploitation. *Man-Environment Systems* 10; 3–10.

Doughty, R. (1981) Environmental theology; trends and prospects in Christian thought. *Progress in Human Geography* 5; 234–48.

Dubos, R. (1972) *A God within*. New York, Scribner.

Dubos, R. (1973) St Francis vs St Benedict. *Psychology Today* 6; 46–53.

Echlin, E. (1989) *The Christian Green heritage; world as creation*. Nottingham, Grove Books.

Eckbo, G. (1987) The city and Nature. *Ekistics*: 325–7.

Ehrenfeld, D. (1978) *The arrogance of humanism*. London, Oxford University Press.

Ehrenfeld, D. and P. J. Bentley (1985) Judaism and the practice of stewardship. *Judaism* 34; 301–11.

Ehrlich, P. and R. Harriman (1971) *How to be a survivor*. London, Pan.

Elder, F. (1970) *Crisis in Eden; a religious study of man and environment*. Nashville, Abingdon.

Elkington, J. & J. Hailes (1988) *The green consumer guide*. London, Gollancz.

Elsdon, R. (1989) A still-bent world; some reflections on current environmental problems. *Science and Christian Belief* 1; 99–122.

Engel, D. E. (1970) Elements in a theology of environment. *Zygon* 5; 216–28.

Ette, A. and R. Waller (1978) The anomaly of a Christian ecology. *Ecologist Quarterly* (Summer); 144–8.

Fackre, G. (1971) Ecology and theology. *Religion in Life* 40; 210–24.

Feenstra, E. S. (1969) The spiritual versus material heresy. *Journal of the American Scientific Affiliation* 29; 44–6.

Flores, D. L. (1983) Zion in Eden; phases of the environmental history of Utah. *Environmental Review* 7; 325–44.

Foley, G. (1988) Deep ecology and subjectivity. *The Ecologist* 18 (4/5); 119–22.

Freudenstein, E. (1970) Ecology and the Jewish tradition. *Judaism* 19; 406–14.

Fritsch, A. J. (1980) *Environmental ethics*. Anchor Press/Doubleday, New York.

Gaebelein, F. E. (1980) Old Testament foundations for living more simply. 27–39 in R. J. Sider (ed) *Living more simply; Biblical principles and practical models*. London, Hodder and Stoughton.

General Synod Board for Social Responsibility (1986) *Our responsibility for the living environment*. London, Church House Publishing.

Glacken, C. J. (1967) *Traces on the Rhodian Shore; nature and culture in western thought from ancient times to the end of the eighteenth century*. Berkeley, University of California Press.

Global 2000 (1980) *Report to the President of the United States*. United States Council on Environmental Quality/Pergamon Press.

Goldsmith, E. (1988) The Way; an ecological world-view. *The Ecologist* 18 (4/5), 160–85.

Gordis, R. (1970) "The earth is the Lord's" – Judaism and the spoliation of nature. *Keeping Posted* XVI; 5–9.

Greig, S., G. Pike and D. Selby (1987) *Earthrights; education as if the planet really mattered*. London, World Wildlife Fund/Kogan Page.

Hasel, G. F. (1974) The polemic nature of the Genesis cosmology. *The Evangelical Quarterly* 46; 81–102.

Helfand, J. (1971) Ecology and the Jewish tradition; a postscript. *Judaism* 20; 330–5.

Hiers, R. (1984) Ecology, Biblical theology, and methodology. *Zygon* 19; 43–59.

Higton, A. (1989) Understanding the New Age Movement. *21CC* (September) 51–3.

Hughes, D. J. (1981) Early Greek and Roman environmentalists. *The Ecologist* 11; 12–20.

Hughes, D. J. (1983) Gaia; an ancient view of our planet. *The Ecologist* 13; 54–60.

Hughes, C. J. (1985) Gaia; a natural scientist's ethic for the future. *The Ecologist* 15; 92–5.

Icke, D. (1990) *It doesn't have to be this way*. Green Books.

Innes, K. (1985) The witness of nature; an Old Testament contribution to Christian spirituality. *New Fire* 8 (64); 418–20.

Innes, K. (1987) *Caring for the earth, the environment, Christians and the church*. Nottingham, Grove Books.

Jacobs, W. R. (1978) The great despoliation; environmental themes in American frontier history. *Pacific Historical Review* 47; 1–26.

Jenkins, S. (1987) *The Bible from scratch*. Tring, Herts., Lion Books.

Kaufman, G. D. (1972) A problem for theology; the concept of nature. *Harvard Theological Review* 65; 337–66.

Kay, J. (1985) Preconditions of natural resource conservation. *Agricultural History* 59; 124–35.

Kay, J. (1988) Concepts of nature in the Hebrew Bible. *Environmental Ethics* 10; 309–27.

Kay, J. (1989) Human dominion over nature in the Hebrew Bible. *Annals of the Association of American Geographers* 79; 214–32.

Kay, J. and C. J. Brown (1985) Mormon beliefs about land and natural resources, 1847–77. *Journal of Historical Geography* 11; 253–67.

Keating, M. (1989) *Toward a common future; a report on sustainable development and its implications for Canada*. Ottawa, Environment Canada 48pp.

Keller, J. A. (1971) Types of motives for ecological concerns. *Zygon* 6; 197–204.

Kumar, S. (1974) The holy world of the Hindus. *Resurgence* 5; 21–2.

LaFreniere, G. L. (1985) World views and environmental ethics. *Environmental Review* 9; 307–22.

Livingstone, D. N. (1983) Environmental theology; prospect in retrospect. *Progress in Human Geography* 7; 133–40.

Lovelock, J. E. (1987) *Gaia; a new look at life on earth.* Oxford, Oxford University Press.

Lowry, P. P. (1971) Toward a radical view of the ecological crisis. *Environmental Affairs* 1; 355.

Lyon, D. (1989) Against the stream 2. Green and pleasant? *Third Way* (Feb); 6–8.

Macquarrie, J. (1971–2) Creation and environment. *Expository Times* lxxxiii; 4–9.

Martin, W. E. (1970) Simple concepts of complex ecological problems. *Zygon* 5; 304–38.

McDonagh, S. (1986) *To care for the earth; a call to a new theology.* London, Chapman.

McDonagh, S. (1990) *The greening of the Church.* London, Chapman.

McHarg, I. L. (1964) The place of nature in the city of man. *Annals of the American Academy of Political and Social Science* 352.

McHarg, I. L. (1971) *Design with nature.* New York, Natural History Press.

McKee, D. (1974) Hands in the soil and heart in prayer. *Resurgence* 5; 15–16.

Meadows, D. *et al* (1972) *The Limits to Growth.* London, Earth Island.

Meyer-Abich, K (1988) quoted in *The New Road* 4, p. 6.

Moltmann, J, (1985) *God in creation.* London, SCM Press.

Moncrief, W. (1970) Cultural basis for our environmental crisis. *Science* 170; 508–12.

Montefiore, H. (1969) *Can man survive?* London, Fontana.

Morris, B. (1981) Changing views of nature. *The Ecologist* 11; 130–7.

Morton, J.P. (1988) Faith for the Planetary Age. *Communities* 75; 51–3.

Moss, R. (1985) The ethical underpinnings of man's management of nature. *Faith and Thought* 111; 23–56.

Myers, N. (ed) (1985) *The Gaia atlas of planet management.* London, Pan.

Myers, N. (1990) Gaia; the lady becomes ever more acceptable. *Geography Review* 3 (3); 3–5.

Naess, A. (1988) Deep Ecology and ultimate premises. *The Ecologist* 18 (4/5); 128–31.

Nicholson, M. (1970) *The environmental revolution.* London; Hodder & Stoughton.

Oakley, F. (1961) Christian theology and the Newtonian science; the rise of the concept of the laws of nature. *Church History* 30; 433–57.

Omo-Fadaka, J. (1974) Ancestor power. *Resurgence* 5; 25.

Ophuls, W. (1977) Buddhist politics. *The Ecologist* 7; 82–6.

Paehlke, R. C. (1989) *Environmentalism and the future of progressive politics.* Cambridge Massachusetts, Yale University Press.

Palmer, M. (1988) *Genesis or nemesis; belief, meaning and ecology.* London, Dryad.

Park, C. C. (1981) *Ecology and environmental management.* London, Butterworth.

Park, C. C. (ed) (1986) *Environmental policies; an international review.* London, Croom Helm.

Park, C. C. (1987) *Acid rain; rhetoric and reality.* London, Methuen.

Park, C. C. (1989) *Chernobyl; the long shadow.* London, Routledge.

Passmore, J. (1974) *Man's responsibility for nature.* New York, Scribner.

Pelcovitz, R. (1970) Ecology and Jewish theology. *Jewish Life* XXXVII 6; 23–32.

Pepper, D. (1984) *The roots of modern environmentalism.* London, Routledge.

Pepper, D. (1987) The basis of a radical curriculum in environmental education. 65–79 in C. Lacey and R. Williams (eds) *Education, ecology and development.* London, World Wildlife Fund/Kogan Page.

Pollard, N. (1984) The Israelites and their environment. *The Ecologist* 14; 125–33.

Porritt, J, (1984) *Seeing green.* Oxford, Blackwell.

Porritt, J. & D. Winner (1988) *The Coming of the Greens*. London, Fontana.

Ratcliffe, D. A. (1976) Thoughts towards a philosophy of nature conservation. *Biological Conservation* 9; 45–53.

Roszak, T. (1971) *The making of a counter-culture; reflections on the technocratic society and its youthful opposition*. London, Faber & Faber.

Roszak, T. (1972) *Where the wasteland ends*. New York, Doubleday.

Royston (1979) *Pollution Prevention Pays*. New York.

von Ruhland, C. (1989) The good earth. *21CC* (September); 22–6.

Runcie, R. (1989) A response to the New Age. *The Church of England Newspaper* 24 November, 15.

Santmire, H. P. (1970) *Brother earth; nature, God and ecology in time of crisis*. New York, Thomas Nelson.

Santmire, H. P. (1975) Reflections on the alleged ecological bankruptcy of western theology. *Anglican Theological Review* LVII (2); 131–52.

Santmire, H. P. (1976) Ecology, justice and theology; beyond the preliminary skirmishes. *Christian Century* XCIII (17); 460–4.

Santmire, H. P. (1980) St Augustine's theology of the biophysical world. *Dialog* 19; 174–85.

Schwarz, H. (1974) The eschatological dimensions of ecology. *Zygon* 9; 323–8.

Schwarz, W. (1990) A whole-earth incarnation. *The Guardian* 12 March; 39.

Schwarzschild, S. S. (1984) The unnatural Jew. *Environmental Ethics* 6; 347–62.

Schumacher, E. F. (1973) *Small is beautiful*. London, Blond & Briggs.

Schumacher, E. F. (1974) Message from the Universe. *Resurgence* 5; 6–8.

Sider, R. J. (ed) (1980) *Living more simply; Biblical principles and practical models*. London, Hodder and Stoughton.

Silva, L. de (1978) Psychological and ethical dimensions of humanity's relation to nature. *Dialogue* 5; 5–12.

Simmons, I. (1988) Our attitudes to life on earth. *Geography Review* (March) 27–30.

Skolimowski, H. (1973) Technology v. nature. *The Ecologist* 3; 50–5.

Skolimowski, H. (1975) Knowledge and values. *The Ecologist* 5; 8–15.

Skolimowski, H. (1981) *Eco-philosophy; designing new tactics for living*. New York, Marion Boyars.

Skolimowski, H. (1988) Eco-Philosophy and Deep Ecology. *The Ecologist* 18 (4/5); 124–7.

Speir, R. (1989) The emergence of Gaia. *Geographical Magazine* December; 30–3.

Spretnak, C. (1986) *The spiritual dimension of green politics*. Santa Fe New Mexico, Bear & Company.

Stott, J. (1989) Conflicting gospels. *Church of England Newspaper* 8 December; 6.

Sylvan, R. and D. Bennett (1988) Taoism and Deep Ecology. *The Ecologist* 18 (4/5); 148–59.

Taylor, P. W. (1981) The ethics of respect for nature. *Environmental Ethics* 3; 197–218.

Toynbee, A. (1974) The religious background of the present environmental crisis. *International Journal of Environmental Studies* 3; 141–6.

Tuan, Yi-Fu (1970) Our treatment of the environment in ideal and actuality. *American Scientist* 58; 244–9.

Tuan, Yi Fu (1974) *Topophilia; a study of environmental perception, attitudes and values*. New Jersey, Prentice Hall.

United Nations Environment Program (1987) *Environmental data report*. Oxford, Blackwell.

Vander Lugt, H. (1990) *Studies in contrasts: the doctrine of Christ*. Grand Rapids, Michigan, Radio Bible Class.

Walter, J.A. (1982) *The human home*. London, Lion.

West, C. (1975) Justice within the limits of the created world. *Ecumenical Review* (Jan); 57–64.

White, L. (1947) Natural science and the naturalistic art in the Middle Ages. *American Historical Review* 52; 433–4.

White, L. (1962) *Medieval Technology and Social Change*. Oxford, Oxford University Press.

White, L. (1967) The historical roots of our ecological crisis. *Science* 155; 1203–7.

Wilkinson, L. (ed) (1980) *Earth keeping; Christian stewardship of natural resources*. Grand Rapids, Eerdmans.

Williams, G. H. (1971) Christian attitudes towards nature – I. *Christian Scholars Review* II; 3–35.

Williams, G. H. (1972) Christian attitudes towards nature – II. *Christian Scholars Review* II; 112–26.

Witt, C. B. de (1988) Christian stewardship. *Communities* 75; 38–40.

World Commission on Environment and Development (1987) *Our Common Future*. Oxford, Oxford University Press.

World Resources Institute (1988) *World resources 1988–9*. London, Basic Books.

Wright, R. T. (1970) Responsibility for the ecological crisis. *BioScience* 20; 851–3.

Wrightsman, B. (1970) Man; manager or manipulator of the earth. *Dialog* 9; 200–14.

The New Army
in Training

The New Army
in Training

by

Rudyard Kipling

UNIFORM
PRESS

Uniform Press Ltd
66 Charlotte Street
London
W1T 4QE

www.uniformpress.co.uk

First published in 1915 by Macmillan and Co.
This edition published in 2015 by Uniform Press Ltd

978-1-910500-04-0

5 4 3 2 1

Printed in India by Imprint Digital
Designed by Charlotte Glyde

CONTENTS

I

II

III

I

MEN AT WORK

'The ore, the furnace and the hammer are all that is needed for a sword.' – Native proverb.

THIS was a cantonment one had never seen before, and the grey-haired military policeman could give no help.

'My experience,' he spoke detachedly, 'is that you'll find everything everywhere. Is it any particular corps you're looking for?'

'Not in the least,' I said.

'Then you're all right. You can't miss getting something.' He pointed generally to the North Camp. 'It's like floods in a town, isn't it?'

He had hit the just word. All known marks in the place were submerged by troops. Parade-grounds to their utmost limits were crowded with them; rises and sky-lines were furred with them, and the length of the roads heaved and rippled like bicycle-chains with blocks of men on the move.

The voice of a sergeant in the torment reserved for sergeants at roll-call boomed across a bunker. He was calling over recruits to a specialist corps.

'But I've called you once!' he snapped at a man in leggings.

'But I'm Clarke Two,' was the virtuous reply.

'Oh, you are, are you?' He pencilled the correction with a scornful mouth, out of one corner of which he added, '"Sloppy" Clarke! You're all Clarkes or Watsons today. You don't know your own names. You don't know what corps you're in. (This was bitterly unjust, for they were squinting up at a biplane.) You don't know anything.'

'Mm!' said the military policeman. 'The more a man has in his head, the harder it is for him to manage his carcass at first. I'm glad I never was a sergeant. Listen to the instructors! Like rooks, ain't it?'

There was a mile of sergeants and instructors, varied by company officers, all at work on the ready material under their hands. They grunted, barked, yapped, expostulated, and, in rare cases, purred, as the lines broke and formed and wheeled over the vast maidan. When companies numbered off one could hear the tone and accent of every walk in life, and maybe half the counties of England, from the deep-throated 'Woon' of the north to the sharp, half-whistled Devonshire 'Tu.' And as the instructors laboured, so did the men, with a passion to learn as passionately as they were taught.

Presently, in the drift of the foot-traffic down the road, there came another grey-haired man, one foot in a bright slipper, which showed he was an old soldier cherishing a sore toe. He drew alongside and considered these zealous myriads.

'Good?' said I, deferentially.

'Yes,' he said, 'Very good' – then, half to himself: 'Quite different, though.' A pivot-man near us had shifted a little, instead of marking time on the wheel. His face clouded, his lips moved. Obviously he was cursing his own clumsiness.

'That's what I meant,' said the veteran, 'Innocent! Innocent! Mark you, they ain't doin' it to be done with it and get off. They're doin' it because – because they want to do it.'

'Wake up! Wake *up* there, Isherwood!' This was a young subaltern's reminder flung at a back which straightened itself. That one human name coming up out of all that maze of impersonal manoeuvring stuck in the memory like wreckage on the ocean.

'An' it wasn't 'ardly even necessary to caution Mister Isherwood,' my companion commented. 'Prob'ly he's bitterly ashamed of 'imself.'

I asked a leading question because the old soldier told me that when his toe was sound, he, too, was a military policeman.

'Crime? Crime?' said he. 'They don't know what crime is – that lot don't – none of 'em!' He mourned over them like a benevolent old Satan looking into a busy Eden, and his last word was 'Innocent!'

The car worked her way through miles of men – men route-marching, going to dig or build bridges, or wrestle with stores and transport – four or five miles of men, and every man with eager eyes. There was no music not even drums and fifes. I heard nothing but a distant skirl of the pipes. Trust a Scot to get his national weapon as long as there is a chief in the North! Admitting that war is a serious business, specially to the man who is being fought for, and that it may be right to carry a long face and contribute to relief funds which should be laid on the National Debt, it surely could do no harm to cheer the men with a few bands. Half the money that has been spent in treating, for example…

THE NORTH IN BLUE

There was a moor among woods with a pond in a hollow, the centre of a world of tents whose population was North-Country. One heard it from far off.

'Yo' mun trail t' pick an' t' rifle at t' same time. Try again,' said the instructor.

An isolated company tried again with set seriousness, and yet again. They were used to the pick – won their living by it, in fact – and so, favoured it more than the rifle; but miners don't carry picks at the trail by instinct, though they can twiddle their rifles as one twiddles walking-sticks.

They were clad in a blue garb that disguised all contours; yet their shoulders, backs, and loins could not altogether be disguised, and these were excellent. Another company, at physical drill in shirt and trousers, showed what superb material had offered itself to be worked upon, and how much poise and directed strength had been added to that material in the past few months. When the New Army gets all its new uniform, it will gaze at itself like a new Narcissus. But the present kit is indescribable. That is why, English fashion, it has been made honourable by its wearers; and our world in the years to come will look back with reverence as well as affection on those blue slops and that epileptic cap. One far-seeing commandant who had special facilities has possessed himself of brass buttons, thousands of 'em, which he has added to his men's outfit for the moral effect of (a) having something to clean, and (b) of keeping it so. It has paid. The smartest regiment in the Service could not do itself justice in such garments, but I managed to get a view of a battalion, coming in from a walk, at a distance which more or less subdued the – er – uniform, and they moved with the elastic swing and little quick ripple that means so much. A miner is not supposed to be as good a marcher as a townsman, but when he gets set to time and pace and learns due economy of effort, his developed back and shoulder muscles take him along very handsomely. Another battalion fell in for parade while I watched, again at a distance. They came to hand quietly and collectedly enough, and with only that amount of pressing which is caused by fear of being late. A platoon – or whatever they call it – was giving the whole of its attention to its signalling instructors, with the air of men resolved on getting the last flicker of the last cinema-film for their money. Crime in the military sense they do not know any more than their fellow-innocents up the road. It is hopeless to pretend to be other than what one is, because one's soul in this life is as exposed as one's body. It is futile to tell civilian lies – there are no civilians to listen – and they have not yet learned to tell Service ones without being detected. It is useless to sulk at any external condition of affairs, because the rest of the world with which a man is concerned is facing those

11

identical conditions. There is neither poverty nor riches, nor any possibility of pride, except in so far as one may do one's task a little better than one's mate.

DUTIES AND DEVELOPMENTS

In the point of food they are extremely well looked after, quality and quantity, wet canteen and dry. Drafts come in all round the clock, and they have to be fed; late guards and sentries want something hot at odd times, and the big marquee-canteen is the world's gathering-place, where food, life's first interest to man in hard work, is thoroughly discussed. They can get outside of a vast o' vittles. Thus, a contractor who delivers ten thousand rations a day stands, by deputy at least, in the presence of just that number of rather fit, long, deep men. They are what is called 'independent' – a civilian weakness which they will learn to blush over in a few months, and to discourage among later recruits; but they are also very quick to pick up dodges and tricks that make a man more comfortable in camp life, and their domestic routine runs on wheels. It must have been hard at first for civilians to see the necessity for that continuous, apparently pernickity, house-maiding and 'following-up' which is vital to the comfort of large bodies of men in confined quarters. In civil life men leave these things to their womenfolk, but where women are not, officers, inspecting tents, feet, and such-like, develop a she-side to their head, and evidently make their non-commissioned officers and men develop it too. A good soldier is always a bit of an old maid. But, as I heard a private say to a sergeant in the matter of some kit chucked into a corner: 'Yo' canna keep owt redd up ony proper gate on a sand-hill' To whom his superior officer: 'Ah know yo' canna', but yo' mun try, Billy.'

And Heaven knows they are trying hard enough – men, N.C.O.'s, and officers with all the masked and undervoiced effort of our peoples when we are really at work. They stand at the very beginning of things; creating out of chaos, meeting emergencies as they arise; handicapped in every direction, and overcoming every handicap by simple goodwill, humour, self-sacrifice, common-sense, and such trumpery virtues. I watched their faces in the camp, and at lunch looked down a line of some twenty men in the mess-tent, wondering how many would survive to see the full splendour and significance of the work here so nobly begun. But they were not interested in the future beyond their next immediate job. They ate quickly and went out to it, and by the time I drove away again I was overtaking their battalions on the road. Not unrelated units lugged together for foot-slogging, but real battalions, of a spirit in themselves which defied even the blue slops – wave after wave of proper men, with undistracted eyes, who never talked a word about any war. But not a note of music and they North-countrymen!

II

IRON INTO STEEL

'Thanda lohã garam lohe ko marta hai.' – (Cold iron will cut hot iron).

AT the next halt I fell into Scotland – blocks and blocks of it – a world of precise-spoken, thin-lipped men, with keen eyes. They gave me directions which led by friendly stages to the heart of another work of creation and a huge drill-shed where the miniature rifles were busy. Few things are duller than Morris-tube practice in the shed, unless it be judging triangles of error against blank-walls. I thought of the military policeman with the sore toe; for these 'innocents' were visibly enjoying both games. They sighted over the sand-bags with the gravity of surveyors, while the instructors hurled knowledge at them like sling-stones.

'Man, d'ye see your error? Step here, man, and I'll show ye.' Teacher and taught glared at each other like theologians in full debate; for this is the Scot's way of giving and getting knowledge.

At the miniature targets squad after squad rose from beside their deadly-earnest instructors, gathered up their target-cards, and whisperingly compared them, five heads together under a window.

'Aye, that was where I loosed too soon.' 'I misdoubt I took too much o' the foresight.' Not a word of hope and comfort in their achievements. Nothing but calvinistic self-criticism.

These men ran a little smaller than the North-country folk down the road, but in depth of chest, girth of fore-arm, biceps, and neck-measurement they were beautifully level and well up; and the squads at bayonet-practice had their balance, drive, and recover already. As the light failed one noticed the whites of their eyes turning towards their instructors. It reminded one that there is always a touch of the cateran in the most docile Scot, even as the wolf persists in every dog.

'And what about crime?' I demanded.

There was none. They had not joined to play the fool. Occasionally a few unstable souls who have mistaken their vocation try to return to civil life by way of dishonourable discharge, and think it 'funny' to pile up offences. The New Army has no use for those people either, and attends to them on what may be called 'democratic lines', which is all the same as the old barrack-room court-martial. Nor does it suffer fools gladly. There is no time to instruct them. They go to other spheres.

There was, or rather is, a man who intends to join a certain battalion. He joined it once, scraped past the local doctor, and was drafted into the corps, only to be hove out for varicose veins. He went back to his accommodating doctor, repeated the process, and was again rejected. They are waiting for him now in his third incarnation; both sides are equally determined. And there was another Scot who joined, served awhile, and left, as he might have left a pit or a factory. Somehow it occurred to him that explanations were required, so he wrote to his commanding officer from his home address and asked him what he recommended him to do. The C.O., to his infinite credit, wrote back: 'Suppose you rejoin,' which the man did, and no more said. His punishment, of course, will come to him when he realises what he has done. If he does not then perish in his self-contempt (he has a good conceit of himself) he will make one first-rate non-commissioned officer.

WITH ILLUSTRATIONS

I had the luck to meet a Sergeant-Major, who was the Sergeant-Major of one's dreams. He had just had sure information that the kilts for his battalion were coming in a few days, so, after three months' hard work, life smiled upon him. From kilts one naturally went on to the pipes. The battalion had its pipes – a very good set. How did it get them? Well, there was, of course, the Duke. They began with him. And there was a Scots lord concerned with the regiment And there was a leddy of a certain clan connected with the battalion. Hence the pipes. Could anything be simpler or more logical? And when the kilts came the men would be different creatures. Were they good men, I asked. 'Yes. Verra good. Wha's to mislead 'em?' said he.

'Old soldiers,' I suggested, meanly enough. 'Rejoined privates of long ago.'

'Ay, there might have been a few such in the beginning, but they'd be more useful in the Special Reserve Battalions. Our boys are good boys, but, ye'll understand, they've to be handled – just handled a little.' Then a subaltern came in, loaded with regimental forms, and visibly leaning on the Sergeant-Major, who explained, clarified, and referred them on the proper quarters.

'Does the work come back to you?' I asked, for he had been long in pleasant civil employ.

'Ay. It does that. It just does that.' And he addressed the fluttering papers, lists, and notes, with the certainty of an old golfer on a well-known green.

Squads were at bayonet practice in the square. (They like bayonet practice, especially after looking at pictures in the illustrated dailies.) A new draft was being introduced to its rifles. The rest were getting ready for evening parade. They were all in khaki, so one could see how they had come on in the last ten weeks. It was a result the meekest might have been proud of, but the New Army does not cultivate useless emotions. Their officers and their instructors worked over them patiently and coldly and repeatedly, with their souls in the job: and with their soul, mind, and body in the same job the men took – soaked up – the instruction. And that seems to be the note of the New Army.

What the Army Does and Thinks

They have joined for good reason. For that reason they sleep uncomplainingly double thick on barrack floors, or lie like herrings in the tents and sing hymns and other things when they are flooded out. They walk and dig half the day or all the night as required; they wear – though they will not eat – anything that is issued to them; they make themselves an organised and kindly life out of a few acres of dirt and a little canvas; they keep their edge and anneal their discipline under conditions that would depress a fox-terrier and disorganise a champion football team. They ask nothing in return save work and equipment. And being what they are, they thoroughly and unfeignedly enjoy what they are doing; and they purpose to do much more.

But they also think. They think it vile that so many unmarried young men who are not likely to be affected by Government allowances should be so shy about sharing their life. They discuss these young men and their womenfolk by name, and imagine rude punishments for them, suited to their known characters. They discuss, too, their elders who in time past warned them of the sin of soldiering. These men, who live honourably and simply under the triple vow of Obedience, Temperance, and Poverty, recall, not without envy, the sort of life which well-kept moralists lead in the unpicketed, unsentried towns; and it galls them that such folk should continue in comfort and volubility at the expense of good men's lives, or should profit greasily at the end of it all. They stare hard, even in their blue slops, at white-collared, bowler-hatted young men, who, by the way, are just learning to drop their eyes under that gaze. In the third-class railway carriages they hint that they would like explanations from the casual 'nut' and they explain to him wherein his explanations are unconvincing. And when they are home on leave, the slack-jawed son of the local shop-keeper, and the rising nephew of the big banker, and the dumb but cunning carter's lad receive instruction or encouragement suited to their needs and the nation's. The older men and the officers will tell you that if the allowances are made more liberal we shall get all the men we want. But the younger men of the New Army do not worry about allowances or, for that matter, make 'em!

There is a gulf already opening between those who have joined and those who have not; but we shall not know the width and the depth of that gulf till the war is over. The wise youth is he who jumps it now and lands in safety among the trained and armed men.

III

GUNS AND SUPPLY

'Under all and after all the wheel carries everything.' – Proverb.

ONE had known the place for years as a picturesque old house, standing in a peaceful park; had watched the growth of certain young oaks along a new-laid avenue, and applauded the owner's enterprise in turning a stretch of pasture to plough. There are scores of such estates in England which the motorist, through passing so often, comes to look upon almost as his own. In a single day the brackened turf between the oaks and the iron road-fence blossomed into tents, and the drives were all cut up with hoofs and wheels. A little later, one's car sweeping home of warm September nights was stopped by sentries, who asked her name and business; for the owner of that retired house and discreetly wooded park had gone elsewhere in haste, and his estate was taken over by the military.

Later still, one met men and horses arguing with each other for miles about that country-side; or the car would be flung on her brakes by artillery issuing from cross-lanes –

clean batteries jingling off to their work on the Downs, and hungry ones coming back to meals. Every day brought the men and the horses and the weights behind them to a better understanding, till in a little while the car could pass a quarter of a mile of them without having to hoot more than once.

'Why are you so virtuous?' she asked of a section encountered at a blind and brambly corner.

'Why do you obtrude your personality less than an average tax-cart?'

'Because,' said a driver, his arm flung up to keep the untrimmed hedge from sweeping his cap off, 'because those are our blessed orders. We don't do it for love.'

No one accuses the Gunner of maudlin affection for anything except his beasts and his weapons. He hasn't the time. He serves at least three jealous gods – his horse and all its saddlery and harness; his gun, whose least detail of efficiency is more important than men's lives; and, when these have been attended to, the never-ending mystery of his art commands him.

It was a wettish, windy day when I visited the so-long-known house and park. Cock pheasants ducked in and out of trim rhododendron clumps, neat gates opened into sacredly preserved vegetable gardens, the many-coloured leaves of specimen trees pasted themselves stickily against sodden tent walls, and there was a mixture of circus smells from the horse-lines and the faint, civilised breath of chrysanthemums in the potting sheds. The main drive was being relaid with a foot of flint; the other approaches were churned and pitted under the gun wheels and heavy supply wagons. Great breadths of what had been well-kept turf between unbrowsed trees were blanks of slippery brown wetness, dotted with picketed horses and field-kitchens. It was a crazy mixture of stark necessity and manicured luxury, all cheek by jowl, in the undiscriminating rain.

SERVICE CONDITIONS

The cook-houses, store-rooms, forges, and work-shops were collections of tilts, poles, rick-cloths, and odd lumber, beavered together as on service. The officers' mess was a thin, soaked marquee. Less than a hundred yards away were dozens of vacant, well-furnished rooms in the big brick house, of which the Staff furtively occupied one corner. There was accommodation for very many men in its stables and out-houses alone; or the whole building might have been gutted and rearranged for barracks twice over in the last three months. Scattered among the tents were rows of half-built tin sheds, the ready-prepared lumber and the corrugated iron lying beside them, waiting to be pieced together like children's toys. But there were no workmen. I was told that they had come that morning, but had knocked off because it was wet.

'I see. And where are the batteries?' I demanded.

'Out at work, of course. They've been out since seven.'

'How shocking! In this dreadful weather, too!'

'They took some bread and cheese with them. They'll be back about dinner-time if you care to wait. Here's one of our field-kitchens.'

Batteries look after their own stomachs, and are not

catered for by contractors. The cook-house was a wagon-tilt. The wood, being damp, smoked a good deal. One thought of the wide, adequate kitchen ranges and the concrete passages of the service quarters in the big house just behind. One even dared to think Teutonically of the perfectly good panelling and the thick hard-wood floors that could...

'Service conditions, you see,' said my guide, as the cook inspected the baked meats and the men inside the wagon-tilt grated the carrots and prepared the onions. It was old work to them after all these months – done swiftly, with the clean economy of effort that camp life teaches. 'What are these lads when they're at home?' I inquired.

'Londoners chiefly – all sorts and conditions.'

The cook in shirt sleeves made another investigation, and sniffed judicially. He might have been cooking since the Peninsular. He looked at his watch and across towards the park gates. He was responsible for one hundred and sixty rations, and a battery has the habit of saying quite all that it thinks of its food.

'How often do the batteries go out?' I continued.

''Bout five days a week. You see, we're being worked up a little.'

'And have they got plenty of ground to work over?'

'Oh – yes-s.'

'What's the difficulty this time? Birds?'

'No; but we got orders the other day not to go over a golf-course. That rather knocks the bottom out of tactical schemes.'

Perfect shamelessness, like perfect virtue, is impregnable;

and, after all, the lightnings of this war, which have brought
out so much resolve and self-sacrifice, must show up equally
certain souls and institutions that are irredeemable.

The weather took off a little before noon. The carpenters
could have put in a good half-day's work on the sheds, and
even if they had been rained upon they had roofs with fires
awaiting their return. The batteries had none of these things.

THE GUNNER AT HOME

They came in at last far down the park, heralded by that
unmistakable half-grumble, half-grunt of guns on the move.
The picketed horses heard it first, and one of them neighed
long and loud, which proved that he had abandoned civilian
habits. Horses in stables and mews seldom do more than
snicker, even when they are halves of separated pairs. But
these gentlemen had a corporate life of their own now, and
knew what 'pulling together' means.

When a battery comes into camp it 'parks' all six guns at the
appointed place, side by side in one mathematically straight
line, and the accuracy of the alignment is, like ceremonial
drill with the Foot, a fair test of its attainments. The ground
was no treat for parking. Specimen trees and draining ditches
had to be avoided and circumvented. The gunners, their
reins, the guns, the ground, were equally wet, and the slob
dropped away like gruel from the brake-shoes. And they were
Londoners – clerks, mechanics, shop assistants, and delivery
men – anything and everything that you please. But they

were all home and at home in their saddles and seats. They said nothing; their officers said little enough to them. They came in across what had once been turf; wheeled with tight traces; halted, unhooked; the wise teams stumped off to their pickets, and, behold, the six guns were left precisely where they should have been left to the fraction of an inch. You could see the wind blowing the last few drops of wet from each leather muzzle-cover at exactly the same angle. It was all old known evolutions, taken unconsciously in the course of their day's work by men well abreast of it.

'Our men have one advantage,' said a voice. 'As Territorials they were introduced to unmade horses once a year at training. So they've never been accustomed to made horses.'

'And what do the horses say about it all?' I asked, remembering what I had seen on the road in the early days.

'They said a good deal at first, but our chaps could make allowances for 'em. They know now.'

Allah never intended the Gunner to talk. His own arm does that for him. The batteries off-saddled in silence, though one noticed on all sides little quiet caresses between man and beast – affectionate nuzzlings and nose-slappings. Surely the Gunner's relation to his horse is more intimate even than the cavalryman's; for a lost horse only turns cavalry into infantry, but trouble in a gun team may mean death all round. And this is the Gunner's war. The young wet officers said so joyously as they passed to and fro picking up scandal about breast-straps and breechings, examining the collars of ammunition-wagon teams, and listening to remarks on shoes. Local blacksmiths, assisted by the battery itself, do the shoeing. There are master smiths and important farriers, who have cheerfully thrown up good wages to help the game, and their horses reward them by keeping fit. A fair proportion of the horses are aged – there was never a Gunner yet satisfied with his team or its rations till he had left the battery – but they do their work as steadfastly and whole-heartedly as the men. I am persuaded the horses like being in society and working out their daily problems of draught and direction. The English, and Londoners particularly, are the kindest and most reasonable of folk with animals. If it were not our business strictly to underrate ourselves for the next few years, one would say that the Territorial batteries had already done wonders. But perhaps it is better to let it all go with the grudging admission wrung out of a wringing wet bombardier, 'Well, it isn't so dam' bad – considering.'

I left them taking their dinner in mess tins to their tents, with a strenuous afternoon's cleaning-up ahead of them. The big park held some thousands of men. I had seen no more than a few hundreds, and had missed the howitzer-batteries after all.

A cock pheasant chaperoned me down the drive, complaining loudly that where he was used to walk with his ladies under the beech trees, some unsporting people had built a miniature landscape with tiny villages, churches, and factories, and came there daily to point cannon at it.

'Keep away from that place,' said I, 'or you'll find yourself in a field-kitchen.'

'Not me!' he crowed. 'I'm as sacred as golf-courses.'

Mechanism and Mechanics

There was a little town a couple of miles down the road where one used to lunch in the old days, and had the hotel to oneself. Now there are six ever-changing officers in billet there, and the astonished houses quiver all day to traction engines and high-piled lorries. A unit of the Army Service Corps and some mechanical transport lived near the station, and fed the troops for twenty miles around.

'Are your people easy to find?' I asked of a wandering private, with the hands of a sweep, the head of a Christian among lions, and suicide in his eye.

'Well, the A.S.C. are in the Territorial Drill Hall for one thing; and for another you're likely to hear *us*! There's some motors come in from Bulford.' He snorted and passed on, smelling of petrol.

The drill-shed was peace and comfort. The A.S.C. were getting ready there for pay-day and for a concert that evening. Outside in the wind and the occasional rain-spurts, life was different. The Bulford motors and some other crocks sat on a side-road between what had been the local garage and a newly-erected workshop of creaking scaffold-poles and bellying slatting rick-cloths, where a forge glowed and general repairs were being effected. Beneath the motors men lay on their backs and called their friends to pass them spanners, or, for pity's sake, to shove another sack under their mud-wreathed heads.

A corporal, who had been nine years a fitter and seven in a city garage, briefly and briskly outlined the more virulent diseases that develop in Government rolling-stock. (I heard quite a lot about Bulford.) Hollow voices from beneath eviscerated gear-boxes confirmed him. We withdrew to the shelter of the rick-cloth workshop – that corporal, the sergeant who had been a carpenter, with a business of his own, and, incidentally, had served through the Boer War; another sergeant who was a member of the Master Builders' Association; and a private who had also been fitter, chauffeur, and a few other things. The third sergeant, who kept a poultry-farm in Surrey, had some duty elsewhere.

A man at a carpenter's bench was finishing a spoke for a newly-painted cart. He squinted along it.

'That's funny,' said the master builder. 'Of course in his own business he'd chuck his job sooner than do wood-work. But it's *all* funny.'

'What I grudge,' a sergeant struck in, 'is havin' to put mechanics to loading and unloading beef. That's where modified conscription for the beauties that won't roll up'd be useful to *us*. We want hewers of wood, we do. And I'd hew 'em!'

'*I* want that file.' This was a private in a hurry, come from beneath an unspeakable Bulford. Some one asked him musically if he 'would tell his wife in the morning who he was with tonight.'

'You'll find it in the tool-chest.' said the sergeant. It was his own sacred tool-chest which he had contributed to the common stock.

'And what sort of men have you got in this unit?' I asked.

'Every sort you can think of. There isn't a thing you

couldn't have made here if you wanted to. But' – the corporal, who had been a fitter, spoke with fervour – 'you can't expect us to make big-ends, can you? That five-ton Bulford lorry out there in the wet.'

'And she isn't the worst,' said the master builder. 'But it's all part of the game. *And* so funny when you come to think of it. Me painting carts, and certificated plumbers loading frozen beef!'

'What about the discipline?' I asked.

The corporal turned a fitter's eye on me. 'The mechanism is the discipline,' said he, with most profound truth. 'Jockeyin' a sick car on the road is discipline, too. *What* about the discipline?' He turned to the sergeant with the carpenter's chest. There was one sergeant of Regulars, with twenty years' service behind him and a knowledge of human nature. He struck in.

'*You* ought to know. You've just been made corporal,' said that sergeant of Regulars.

'Well, there's so much which everybody knows has got to be done that – that – why, we all turn in and do it,' quoth the corporal. '*I* don't have any trouble with my lot.'

'Yes; that's how the case stands,' said the sergeant of Regulars. 'Come and see our stores.' They were beautifully arranged in a shed which felt like a monastery after the windy, clashing world without; and the young private who acted as checker – he came from some railway office – had the thin, keen face of the cleric.

'We're in billets in the town,' said the sergeant who had been a carpenter. 'But I'm a married man. I shouldn't care

29

to have men billeted on us at home, an' I don't want to inconvenience other people. So I've knocked up a bunk for myself on the premises. It's handier to the stores, too.'

'The Humour of It'

We entered what had been the local garage. The mechanical transport were in full possession, tinkering the gizzards of more cars. We discussed chewed-up gears (samples to hand), and the civil population's old-time views of the military. The corporal told a tale of a clergyman in a Midland town who, only a year ago, on the occasion of some manoeuvres, preached a sermon warning his flock to guard their womenfolk against the soldiers.

'And when you think – when you know,' said the corporal, 'what life in those little towns really is!' He whistled.

'See that old landau,' said he, opening the door of an ancient wreck jammed against a wall. 'That's two of our chaps' dressing-room. They don't care to be billeted, so they sleep 'tween the landau and the wall. It's handier for their work, too. Work comes in at all hours. I wish I was cavalry. There's some use in cursing a horse.'

Truly, it's an awful thing to belong to a service where speech brings no alleviation.

'You!' A private with callipers turned from the bench by the window. 'You'd die outside of a garage. But what you said about civilians and soldiers is all out of date now.'

The sergeant of Regulars permitted himself a small,

hidden smile. The private with the callipers had been some twelve weeks a soldier. 'I don't say it isn't,' said the corporal, 'I'm saying what it used to be.'

'We-ell,' the private screwed up the callipers, 'didn't you feel a little bit that way yourself – when you were a civilian?'

'I – I don't think I did.' The corporal was taken aback. 'I don't think I ever thought about it.'

'Ah! *There* you are!' said the private, very drily.

Some one laughed in the shadow of the landau dressing-room. 'Anyhow, we're all in it now, Private Percy,' said a voice.

There must be a good many thousand conversations of this kind being held all over England nowadays. Our breed does not warble much about patriotism or Fatherland, but it has a wonderful sense of justice, even when its own shortcomings are concerned.

We went over to the drill-shed to see the men paid.

The first man I ran across there was a sergeant who had served in the Mounted Infantry in the South African picnic that we used to call a war. He had been a private chauffeur for some years – long enough to catch the professional look, but was joyously reverting to service type again.

The men lined up, were called out, saluted emphatically at the pay-table, and fell back with their emoluments. They smiled at each other.

'An' it's *all* so funny,' murmured the master builder in my ear. 'About a quarter – no, less than a quarter of what one 'ud be making on one's own!'

'Fifty bob a week, cottage, and all found, I was. An' only two cars to look after,' said a voice behind. 'An' if I'd been asked – simply *asked* – to lie down in the mud all the aftenoon–!' The speaker looked at his wages with awe. Some one wanted to know, *sotto voce*, if 'that was union rates,' and the grin spread among the uniformed experts. The joke, you will observe, lay in situations thrown up, businesses abandoned, and pleasant prospects cut short at the nod of duty.

'Thank Heaven!' said one of them at last, 'it's too dark to work on those blessed Bulfords any more today. We'll get ready for the concert.'

But it was not too dark, half an hour later, for my car to meet a big lorry storming back in the wind and the wet from the northern camps. She gave me London allowance – half one inch between hub and hub – swung her corner like a Brooklands professional, changed gear for the uphill with a sweet click, and charged away. For aught I knew, she was driven by an ex-'fifty-bob-a-week-a-cottage-and-all-found'-er, who next month might be dodging shells with her and thinking it '*all* so funny'.

Horse, Foot, even the Guns may sometimes get a little rest, but so long as men eat thrice a day there is no rest for the Army Service Corps. They carry the campaign on their all-sustaining backs.

IV

CANADIANS IN CAMP

'Before you hit the buffalo, find out where the rest of the herd is.' – Proverb

THIS particular fold of downs behind Salisbury might have been a hump of prairie near Winnipeg. The team that came over the rise, widely spaced between pole-bar and whiffle-trees, were certainly children of the prairie. They shied at the car. Their driver asked them dispassionately what they thought they were doing, anyway. They put their wise heads together, and did nothing at all. Yes. Oh, yes! said the driver. They were Western horses. They weighed better than twelve hundred apiece. He himself was from Edmonton way. The Camp? Why, the camp was right ahead along up this road. No chance to miss it, and, 'Sa-ay! Look out for our lorries!'

A fleet of them hove in sight going at the rate of knots, and keeping their left with a conscientiousness only learned when you come out of a country where nearly all the Provinces (except British Columbia) keep to the right. Every line of them, from steering-wheel to brake-shoes, proclaimed their nationality. Three perfectly efficient young men who were sprinkling a golf green with sifted earth ceased their duties to stare at them. Two riding-boys (also efficient) on racehorses, their knees under their chins and their saddles between their horses' ears, cantered past on the turf. The rattle of the motors upset their catsmeat, so one could compare their style of riding with that of an officer loping along to over-take a string of buck-wagons that were trotting towards the horizon. The riding-boys have to endure sore hardship nowadays. One gentleman has already complained that his 'private gallops' are being cut up by gun-wheels and 'irremediably ruined.'

Then more lorries, contractors' wagons, and increasing vileness of the battered road-bed, till one slid through a rude gate into a new world, of canvas as far as the eye could reach, and beyond that outlying clouds of tents. It is not a contingent that Canada has sent, but an army – horse, foot, guns, engineers, and all details, fully equipped. Taking that army's strength at thirty-three thousand, and the Dominion's population at eight million, the camp is Canada on the scale of one to two hundred and forty – an entire nation unrolled across a few square miles of turf and tents and huts. Here I could study at close hand 'a Colony' yearning to shake off 'the British yoke.' For, beyond question, they yearned – the rank and file unreservedly, the officers with more restraint but equal fervour – and the things they said about the Yoke were simply lamentable.

From Nova Scotia to Victoria, and every city, township, distributing-centre, and divisional point between; from subtropical White River and sultry Jackfish to the ultimate north that lies up beside Alaska; from Kootenay, and Nelson of the fruit-farms, to Prince Edward Island, where motors are not allowed; they yearned to shake it off, with the dust of England from their feet, 'at once and some time before that'.

I had been warned that when Armageddon came the 'Colonies' would 'revolt against the Mother Country as one man'; but I had no notion I should ever see the dread spectacle with my own eyes or the 'one man' so tall!

Joking apart, the Canadian Army wants to get to work. It admits that London is 'some city,' but says it did not take the trip to visit London only. Armageddon, which so many people in Europe knew was bound to come, has struck Canada out of the blue, like a noonday murder in a small town. How will they feel when they actually view some of the destruction in France, these men who are used to making and owning their homes? And what effect will it have on their land's outlook and development for the next few generations? Older countries may possibly slip back into some sort of toleration. New peoples, in their first serious war, like girls in their first real love-affair, neither forget nor forgive. That is why it pays to keep friends with the young.

And such young! They ran inches above all normal standards, not in a few companies or battalions, but through the whole corps; and it was not easy to pick out foolish or even dull faces among them. Details going about their business through the camp's much mud; defaulters on fatigue;

orderlies, foot and mounted; the procession of lorry-drivers; companies falling in for inspection; battalions parading; brigades moving off for manoeuvres; batteries clanking in from the ranges; they were all supple, free, and intelligent; and moved with a lift and a drive that made one sing for joy.

CAMP GOSSIP

Only a few months ago that entire collection poured into Valcartier camp in pink shirts and straw hats, desperately afraid they might not be in time. Since then they have been taught several things. Notably, that the more independent the individual soldier, the more does he need forethought and endless care when he is in bulk.

'Just because we were all used to looking after ourselves in civil life,' said an officer, 'we used to send parties out without rations. And the parties used to go, too! And we expected the boys to look after their own feet. But we're wiser now.'

'They're learning the same thing in the New Army,' I said. 'Company officers have to be taught to be mothers and housekeepers and sanitary-inspectors. Where do your men come from?'

'Tell me some place that they don't come from,' said he, and I could not. The men had rolled up from everywhere between the Arctic circle and the border, and I was told that those who could not get into the first contingent were moving heaven and earth and local politicians to get into the second.

'There's some use in politics now,' that officer reflected.

'But it's going to thin the voting-lists at home.'

A good many of the old South African crowd (the rest are coming) were present and awfully correct. Men last met as privates between De Aar and Belmont were captains and majors now, while one lad who, to the best of his ability, had painted Cape Town pink in those fresh years, was a grim non-commissioned officer worth his disciplined weight in dollars.

'I didn't remind Dan of old times when he turned up at Valcartier disguised as a respectable citizen,' said my informant. 'I just roped him in for my crowd. He's a father to 'em. He knows.'

'And have you many cheery souls coming on?' I asked.

'Not many; but it's always the same with a first contingent. You take everything that offers and weed the bravoes out later.'

'*We* don't weed,' said an officer of artillery. 'Any one who has had his passage paid for by the Canadian Government stays with us till he eats out of our hand. *And* he does. They make the best men in the long run,' he added. I thought of a friend of mine who is now disabusing two or three 'old soldiers' in a Service corps of the idea that they can run the battalion, and I laughed. The Gunner was right. 'Old soldiers' after a little loving care, become valuable and virtuous.

A company of Foot was drawn up under the lee of a fir plantation behind us. They were a miniature of their army as their army was of their people, and one could feel the impact of strong personality almost like a blow.

'If you'd believe it,' said a cavalryman, 'we're forbidden to cut into that little wood-lot, yonder! Not one stick of it may we have! We could make shelters for our horses in a day out of that stuff.'

'But it's timber!' I gasped. 'Sacred, tame trees!'

'Oh, we know what wood is! They issue it to us by the pound. Wood to burn by the pound! What's wood for, anyway?'

'And when do you think we shall be allowed to go?' someone asked, not for the first time.

'By and by,' said I. 'And then you'll have to detail half your army to see that your equipment isn't stolen from you.'

'What!' cried an old Strathcona Horse. He looked anxiously towards the horse-lines.

'I was thinking of your mechanical transport and your travelling workshops and a few other things that you've got.'

I got away from those large men on their windy hill-top, and slid through mud and past mechanical transport and troops untold towards Lark Hill. On the way I passed three fresh-cut pine sticks, laid and notched one atop of the other to shore up a caving bank. Trust a Canadian or a beaver within gunshot of standing timber!

ENGINEERS AND APPLIANCES

Lark Hill is where the Canadian Engineers live, in the midst of a profligate abundance of tools and carts, pontoon wagons, field telephones, and other mouth-watering gear. Hundreds of tin huts are being built there, but quite leisurely, by contract. I noticed three workmen, at eleven o'clock of that Monday forenoon, as drunk as Davy's sow, reeling and shouting across the landscape. So far as I could ascertain, the workmen do not work extra shifts, nor even, but I hope this is incorrect, on Saturday afternoons; and I think they take their full hour at noon these short days.

Every camp throws up men one has met at the other end of the earth; so, of course, the Engineer C.O. was an ex-South African Canadian.

'Some of our boys are digging a trench over yonder,' he said. 'I'd like you to look at 'em.' The boys seemed to average five feet ten inches, with thirty-seven inch chests. The soil was unaccommodating chalk.

'What are you?' I asked of the first pickaxe.

'Private.'

'Yes, but before that?'

'McGill (University understood). Nineteen twelve.'

'And that boy with the shovel?'

'Queen's, I think. No; he's Toronto.'

And thus the class in applied geology went on half up the trench, under supervision of a Corporal-Bachelor-of-Science with a most scientific biceps. They were young; they were beautifully fit, and they were all truly thankful that they lived in these high days.

Sappers, like sergeants, take care to make themselves comfortable. The corps were dealing with all sorts of little domestic matters in the way of arrangements for baths, which are cruelly needed, and an apparatus for depopulating shirts, which is even more wanted. Healthy but unwashen men sleeping on the ground are bound to develop certain things which at first disgust them, but later are accepted as an unlovely part of the game. It would be quite easy to make bakehouses and super-heated steam fittings to deal with the trouble. The huts themselves stand on brick piers, from one to three feet above ground. The board floors are not grooved or tongued, so there is ample ventilation from beneath; but they have installed decent cooking ranges and gas, and the men have already made themselves all sorts of handy little labour-saving gadgets. They would do this if they were in the real desert. Incidentally, I came across a delightful bit of racial instinct. A man had been told to knock up a desk out of broken packing-cases. There is only one type of desk in Canada – the roller-top, with three shelves each side the knee-hole, characteristic sloping sides, raised back, and long shelf in front of the writer. He reproduced it faithfully, barring, of course, the roller-top; and the thing leaped to the eye out of its English office surroundings. The Engineers do not suffer for lack of talents. Their senior officers appear to have been the heads, and their juniors the assistants, in big concerns that wrestle with unharnessed nature. (There is a tale of the building of a bridge in Valcartier Camp which is not bad hearing.) The rank and file include miners; road, trestle, and bridge men; iron construction men who, among other things, are steeplejacks; whole castes of such as deal in high explosives for a living; loco-drivers, superintendents, too, for aught I know, and a solid packing of selected machinists, mechanics, and electricians. Unluckily, they were all a foot or so too tall for me to tell them that, even if their equipment escaped at the front, they would infallibly be raided for their men.

An Unrelated Detachment

I left McGill, Queen's, and Toronto still digging in their trench, which another undergraduate, mounted and leading a horse, went out of his way to jump standing. My last glimpse was of a little detachment, with five or six South African ribbons among them, who were being looked over by an officer. No one thought it strange that they should have embodied themselves and crossed the salt seas independently as 'So-and-So's Horse'. (It is best to travel with a title these days.) Once arrived, they were not at all particular, except that they meant to join the Army, and the lonely batch was stating its qualifications as Engineers.

'They get over any way and every way,' said my companion. 'Swimming, I believe.'

'But who was the So-and-So that they were christened after?' I asked.

'I guess he was the man who financed 'em or grub-staked 'em while they were waiting. He may be one of 'em in that crowd now; or he may be a provincial magnate at home getting another bunch together.'

The Vanguard of a Nation

Then I went back to the main camp for a last look at that wonderful army, where the tin-roofed messes take French conversation lessons with the keen-faced French-Canadian officers, and where one sees esprit-de-Corps in the making.

41

Nowhere is local sentiment stronger than in Canada. East and West, lake and maritime provinces, prairie and mountain, fruit district and timber lands – they each thrill to it. The West keeps one cold blue open-air eye on the townful East. Winnipeg sits between, posing alternately as sophisticated metropolis and simple prairie. Alberta, of the thousand horses, looks down from her high-peaked saddle on all who walk on their feet; and British Columbia thanks God for an equable climate, and that she is not like Ottawa, full of politicians and frozen sludge. Quebec, unassailable in her years and experience, smiles tolerantly on the Nova Scotian, for he has a history too, and asks Montreal if any good thing can come out of Brandon, Moose Jaw, or Regina. They discuss each other outrageously, as they know each other intimately, over four thousand miles of longitude – their fathers, their families, and all the connections. Which is useful when it comes to sizing up the merits of a newly-promoted non-commissioned officer or the capacities of a quartermaster.

As their Army does and suffers, and its record begins to blaze, fierce pride of regiment will be added to local love and the national pride that backs and envelops all. But that pride is held in very severe check now; for they are neither provinces nor tribes but a welded people fighting in the War of Liberty. They permit themselves to hope that the physique of their next contingent will not be worse than that of the present. They believe that their country can send forward a certain number of men and a certain number behind that, all equipped to a certain scale. Of discomforts endured, of the long learning and relearning and waiting on, they say nothing.

They do not hint what they will do when their hour strikes, though they more than hint their longing for that hour. In all their talk I caught no phrase that could be twisted into the shadow of a boast or any claim to superiority, even in respect to their kit and outfit; no word or implication of self-praise for any sacrifice made or intended. It was their rigid humility that impressed one as most significant and, perhaps, most menacing for such as may have to deal with this vanguard of an armed Nation.

V

INDIAN TROOPS

'Larai meñ laddu nahiñ batte' (War is not sugar-plums).
– Hindi Proverb.

WORKING from the East to the West of England, through a countryside alive with troops of all arms, the car came at dusk into a cathedral town entirely inhabited by one type of regiment. The telegraph-office was an orderly jam of solid, large, made men, with years of discipline behind them and the tan of Indian suns on their faces – Englishmen still so fresh from the troopships that one of them asked me, 'What's the day o' the month?' They were advising friends of their arrival in England, or when they might be expected on short leave at the week's end; and the fresh-faced telegraph girls behind the grilles worked with six pairs of hands apiece and all the goodwill and patience in the world to back them. That same young woman who, with nothing to do, makes you wait ten minutes for a penny stamp while she finishes a talk with a lady-friend, will, at a crisis, go on till she drops,

44

and keep her temper throughout. 'Well, *if* that's her village,' I heard one of the girls say to an anxious soul, 'I tell *you* that that will be her telegraph-office. You leave it to me. *She'll* get it all right.'

He backed out, and a dozen more quietly took his place. Their regiments hailed from all the old known stations of the East and beyond that into the Far East again. They cursed their cool barrack accommodation; they rejoiced in the keen autumn smells, and paraded the long street all filled with 'Europe shops'; while their officers and their officers' wives, and, I think, mothers who had come down to snatch a glimpse of their boys, crowded the hotels, and the little unastonished Anglo-Indian children circulated round the knees of big friends they had made aboardship and asked, 'Where are you going now?'

One caught scraps of our old gipsy talk – names of boarding-houses, agents' addresses: 'Milly stays with mother, of course.' 'I'm taking Jack down to school tomorrow. It's past half-term, but that doesn't matter nowadays'; and cheery farewells between men and calm-eyed women. Except for the frocks, it might have been an evening assembly at any station bandstand in India.

Outside, on the surging pavements, a small boy cried: 'Paper! Evenin' paper!' Then seductively, '*Kargus*!'

'What?' I said, thinking my ears had cheated me.

'*Dekko! Kargus!*' said he. ('Look here! Paper!')

'Why on earth d'you say that?'

'Because the men like it,' he replied, and slapped an evening paper (no change for a penny) into the hand of a

45

man in a helmet.

Who shall say that the English are not adaptable?

The car swam bonnet-deep through a mile of troops; and a mile up the road one could hear the deep hum of all those crowded streets that the cathedral bells were chiming over. It was only one small block of Anglo-India getting ready to take its place in the all-devouring Line.

SCREW-GUNS

An hour later at —— (Shall we ever be able to name people and places outright again?) the wind brought up one whiff – one unmistakable whiff – of *ghi*. Somewhere among the English pines that, for the moment, pretended to be the lower slopes of the Dun, there were native troops. A mule squealed in the dark and set off half-a-dozen others. It was screw-guns – batteries of them, waiting their turn also at the game. Morning showed them in their immaculate lines as though they had just marched in from Jutogh – little, low guns with their ammunition; very big English gunners in disengaged attitudes which, nevertheless, did not encourage stray civilians to poke and peer into things; and the native drivers all busied over their charges. True, the wind was bitter, and many of the drivers had tied up their heads, but so one does at Quetta in the cold weather – not to mention Peshawur – and, said a naick of drivers: 'It is not the cold for which we have no liking. It is the wet. The English air is good, but water falls at all seasons. Yet notwithstanding, we of this battery (and, oh, the pride men can throw into a mere number!) have not lost one mule. Neither at sea nor on land have we *one* lost. That can be shown, sahib.'

Then one heard the deep racking tobacco-cough in the lee of a tent where four or five men – Kangra folk by the look of them – were drinking tobacco out of a cow's horn. Their own country's tobacco, be sure, for English tobacco… but there was no need to explain. Who would have dreamed to smell bazaar-tobacco on a south country golf links?

A large proportion of the men are, of course, Sikhs, to whom tobacco is forbidden; the Havildar Major himself was a Sikh of the Sikhs. He spoke, of all things in this strange world, of the late Mr. M. McAuliffe's monumental book on the Sikh religion, saying, not without warrant, that McAuliffe Sahib had translated into English much of the Holy Book – the great Grunth Sahib that lives at Amritzar. He enlarged, too, on the ancient prophecy among the Sikhs – that a hatted race should some day come out of the sea and lead them to victory all the earth over. So spoke Bir Singh, erect and enormous beneath the grey English skies. He hailed from a certain place called Banalu, near Patiala, where many years ago two Sikh soldiers executed a striking but perfectly just vengeance on certain villagers who had oppressed their young brother, a cultivator. They had gone to the extreme limits of abasement and conciliation. This failing, they took leave for a week-end and slew the whole tribe of their enemies. The story is buried in old Government reports, but when Bir Singh implied that he and his folk were orthodox I had no doubt of it. And behind him stood another giant, who knew, for his village was but a few miles up the Shalimar road, every foot of Lahore city. He brought word that there had been great floods at home, so that the risen Ravi river had touched the very walls of Runjit Singh's Fort. And that was only last rains – and, behold! – here he was now in England waiting orders to go to this fight which, he understood, was not at all a small fight, but a fight of fights, in which all the world and 'our Raj' was engaged. The trouble in India was that all the young men – the mere *jiwan*s – wanted to come out at once, which, he said, was manifestly unjust to older men, who had waited so long. However, merit and patience had secured their reward, and the battery was here, and it would do the hot *jiwans* no harm to stay at home, and be zealous at drill until orders came for them in their turn. 'Young men think that everything good in this world is theirs by right, sahib.'

Then came the big, still English gunners, who are trained to play with the little guns. They took one such gun and melted it into trifling pieces of not more than a hundred and fifty pounds each, and reassembled it, and explained its innermost heart till even a layman could understand. There is a lot to understand about screw-guns – specially the new kind. But the gunner of today, like his ancestor, does not talk much, except in his own time and place, when he is as multitudinously amazing as the Blue Marine.

THE MULE LINES

We went over to see the mule lines. I detest the whole generation of these parrot-mouthed hybrids, American, Egyptian, Andalusian, or up-country: so it gave me particular pleasure to hear a Pathan telling one chestnut beast who objected to having its mane hogged any more, what sort of lady-horse his mamma had been. But *qua* animals, they were a lovely lot, and had long since given up blowing and finicking over English fodder.

'Is there any sickness? Why is yonder mule lying down?' I demanded, as though all the lines could not see I was a shuddering amateur.

'There is no sickness, sahib? That mule lies down for his own pleasure. Also, to get out of the wind. He is very clever. He is from Hindustan,' said the man with the horse-clippers.

'And thou?'

'I am a Pathan,' said he with impudent grin and true border cock of the turban, and he did me the honour to let me infer.

The lines were full of talk as the men went over their animals. They were not worrying themselves over this new country of Belait. It was the regular gossip of food and water and firewood, and where so-and-so had hid the curry-comb.

Talking of cookery, the orthodox men have been rather put out by English visitors who come to the cook-houses and stare directly at the food while it is being prepared. Sensible men do not object to this, because they know that these Englishmen have no evil intention nor any evil eye; but sometimes a narrow-souled purist (toothache or liver makes a man painfully religious) will 'spy strangers' and insist on the strict letter of the law, and then every one who wishes to be orthodox must agree with him – on an empty stomach, too – and wait till a fresh mess has been cooked. This is *taklif* – a burden – for where the intention is good and war is afoot much can and should be overlooked. Moreover, this war is not like any other war. It is a war of *our* Raj – 'everybody's war,' as they say in the bazaars. And that is another reason why it does not matter if an Englishman stares at one's food. This I gathered in small pieces after watering time when the mules had filed up to the troughs in the twilight, hundreds of them, and the drivers grew discursive on the way to the lines.

The last I saw of them was in the early cold morning, all in marching order, jinking and jingling down a road through woods.

'Where are you going?'

'God knows!'

THE INN OF GOOD-BYES

It might have been for exercise merely, or it might be down to the sea and away to the front for the battle of 'Our Raj'. The quiet hotel where people sit together and talk in earnest strained pairs is well used to such departures. The officers of a whole Division – the raw cuts of their tent-circles lie still unhealed on the links – dined there by scores; mothers and relatives came down from the uttermost parts of Scotland for a last look at their boys, and found beds goodness knows where: very quiet little weddings, too, set out from its doors to the church opposite. The Division went away a century of weeks ago by the road that the mule-battery took. Many of the civilians who pocketed the wills signed and witnessed in the smoking-room are full-blown executors now; some of the brides are widows.

And it is not nice to remember that when the hotel was so filled that not even another pleading mother could be given a place in which to lie down and have her cry out – not at all nice to remember that it never occurred to any of the comfortable people in the large but sparsely inhabited houses around that they might have offered a night's lodging, even to an unintroduced stranger.

GREATHEART AND CHRISTIANA

There were hospitals up the road preparing and being prepared for the Indian wounded. In one of these lay a man of, say, a Biluch regiment, sorely hit. Word had come from his colonel in France to the colonel's wife in England that she should seek till she found that very man and got news from his very mouth – news to send to his family and village. She found him at last, and he was very bewildered to see her there, because he had left her and her child on the verandah of the bungalow, long and long ago, when he and his colonel and the regiment went down to take ship for the war. How had she come? Who had guarded her during her train-journey of so many days? And, above all, how had the baba endured that sea which caused strong men to collapse? Not till all these matters had been cleared up in fullest detail did Greatheart on his cot permit his colonel's wife to waste one word on his own insignificant concerns. And that she should have wept filled him with real trouble. Truly, this is the war of 'Our Raj!'

VI

TERRITORIAL BATTALIONS

'To excuse oneself to oneself is human: but to excuse oneself to one's children is Hell.' – Arabic Proverb.

BILLETED troops are difficult to get at. There are thousands of them in a little old town by the side of an even older park up the London Road, but to find a particular battalion is like ferreting unstopped burrows.

'The Umpty-Umpth, were you looking for?' said a private in charge of a side-car, 'We're the Eenty-Eenth. Only came in last week, I've never seen this place before. It's pretty. Hold on! There's a postman. He'll know.'

He, too, was in khaki, bowed between mail-bags, and his accent was of a far and coaly county.

'I'm none too sure,' said he, 'but I think I saw – '

Here a third man cut in.

'Yon's t' battalion, marchin' into t' park now. Roon! Happen tha'll catch 'em.'

They turned out to be Territorials with a history behind

them; but that I didn't know till later; and their band and cyclists. Very polite were those rear-rank cyclists – who pushed their loaded machines with one vast hand apiece.

They were strangers, they said. They had only come here a few days ago. But they knew the South well. They had been in Gloucestershire, which was a very nice southern place. Then their battalion, I hazarded, was of northern extraction? They admitted that I might go as far as that; their speech betraying their native town at every rich word.

'Huddersfield, of course?' I said, to make them out with it.

'Bolton,' said one at last. Being in uniform the pitman could not destroy the impertinent civilian.

'Ah, Bolton!' I returned. 'All cotton, aren't you?'

'Some coal,' he answered gravely. There is notorious rivalry 'twixt coal and cotton in Bolton, but I wanted to see him practise the self-control that the Army is always teaching.

As I have said, he and his companion were most polite, but the total of their information, boiled and peeled, was that they had just come from Bolton way; might at any moment be sent somewhere else, and they liked Gloucestershire in the south. A spy could not have learned much less.

The battalion halted, and moved off by companies for further evolutions. One could see they were more than used to drill and arms; a hardened, thick-necked, thin-flanked, deep-chested lot, dealt with quite faithfully by their sergeants, and altogether abreast of their work. Why, then, this reticence? What had they to be ashamed of, these big Bolton folk without an address? Where was their orderly-room?

There were many orderly rooms in the little old town,

most of them in bye-lanes less than one car wide. I found what I wanted, and this was north country all over – a private who volunteered to steer me to headquarters through the tricky southern streets. He was communicative, and told me a good deal about typhoid inoculation and musketry practice, which accounted for only six companies being on parade. But surely they could not have been ashamed of *that*.

GUARDING A RAILWAY

I unearthed their skeleton at last in a peaceful, gracious five-hundred-year-old house that looked on to lawns and cut hedges bounded by age-old red brick walls – such a perfumed and dreaming place as one would choose for the setting of some even-pulsed English love-tale of the days before the war.

Officers were billeted in the low-ceilinged, shiny-floored rooms full of books and flowers.

'And now,' I asked, when I had told the tale of the uncommunicative cyclist, 'what is the matter with your battalion?'

They laughed cruelly at me. 'Matter!' said they. 'We're just off three months of guarding railways. After *that* a man wouldn't trust his own mother. You don't mean to say our cyclists let you know where we've come from last?'

'No, they didn't,' I replied. 'That was what worried me. I assumed you'd all committed murders, and had been sent here to live it down.'

Then they told me what guarding a line really means. How men wake and walk, with only express troop-trains to keep them company, all the night long on windy embankments or under still more windy bridges; how they sleep behind three sleepers up-ended or a bit of tin, or, if they are lucky, in a platelayer's hut; how their food comes to them slopping across the square-headed ties that lie in wait to twist a man's ankle after dark; how they stand in blown coal-dust of goods-yards trying to watch five lines of trucks at once; how fools of all classes pester the lonely pickets, whose orders are to hold up motors for inquiry, and then write silly letters to the War Office about it. How nothing ever happens through the long weeks but infallibly would if the patrols were taken off. And they had one refreshing story of a workman who at six in the morning, which is no auspicious hour to jest with Lancashire, took a short cut to his work by ducking under some goods-wagons, and when challenged by the sentry replied, posturing on all fours, 'Boo, I'm a German!' Whereat the upright sentry fired, unfortunately missed him, and then gave him the butt across his ass's head, so that his humour, and very nearly his life, terminated. After which the sentry was seldom seen to smile, but frequently heard to murmur, 'Ah should hev slipped t' baggonet into him.'

PRIDE AND PREJUDICE

'So you see,' said the officers in conclusion, 'you mustn't be surprised that our men wouldn't tell you much.'

'I begin to see,' I said. 'How many of you are coal and how

many cotton?'

'Two-thirds coal and one-third cotton, roughly. It keeps the men deadly keen. An operative isn't going to give up while a pitman goes on; and very much *vice versa*.'

'That's class-prejudice,' said I.

'It's most useful,' said they. The officers themselves seemed to be interested in coal or cotton, and had known their men intimately on the civil side. If your orderly-room sergeant, or your quarter-master has been your trusted head clerk or foreman for ten or twelve years, and if eight out of a dozen sergeants have controlled pitmen and machinists, above and below ground, and eighty per cent of these pitmen and machinists are privates in the companies, your regiment works with something of the precision of a big business.

It was all new talk to me, for I had not yet met a Northern Territorial battalion with the strong pride of its strong town behind it. Where were they when the war came? How had they equipped themselves? I wanted to hear the tale. It was worth listening to as told with North-Country joy of life and the doing of things in that soft down-country house of the untroubled centuries. Like every one else, they were expecting anything but war. Hadn't even begun their annual camp. Then the thing came, and Bolton rose as one man and woman to fit out its battalion. There was a lady who wanted a fairly large sum of money for the men's extra footgear. She set aside a morning to collect it, and inside the hour came home with nearly twice her needs, and spent the rest of the time trying to make people take back fivers, at least, out of tenners. And the big hauling firms flung horses and transport at them and at the Government, often refusing any price, or, when it was paid, turning it into the war funds. What the battalion wanted it had but to ask for. Once it was short of, say, towels. An officer approached the head of a big firm, with no particular idea he would get more than a few dozen from that quarter.

'And how many towels d'you want?' said the head of the firm. The officer suggested a globular thousand.

'I think you'll do better with twelve hundred,' was the curt answer. 'They're ready out yonder. Get 'em.'

And in this style Bolton turned out her battalion. Then the authorities took it and strung it by threes and fives along several score miles of railway track: and it had only just been reassembled, and it had been inoculated for typhoid. Consequently, they said (but all officers are like mothers and motorcar owners), it wasn't up to what it would be in a little time. In spite of the cyclist, I had had a good look at the deep-chested battalion in the park, and after getting their musketry figures,[1] it seemed to me that very soon it might be worth looking at by more prejudiced persons than myself.

The next day I read that this battalion's regular battalion in the field had distinguished itself by a piece of work which, in other wars, would have been judged heroic. Bolton will read

[1]Thanks to the miniature rifle clubs fostered by Lord Roberts, a certain number of recruits in all the armies come to their regiments with a certain knowledge of sighting, rifle-handling, and the general details of good shooting, especially at snap and disappearing work.

it, not without remarks, and other towns who love Bolton, more or less, will say that if all the truth could come out their regiments had done as well. Anyway, the result will be more men – pitmen, millhands, clerks, checkers, weighers, winders, and hundreds of those sleek, well-groomed business-chaps whom one used to meet in the big Midland hotels, protesting that war was out of date. These latter develop surprisingly in the camp atmosphere. I recall one raging in his army shirt-sleeves at a comrade who had derided his principles. 'I *am* a blanky pacificist,' he hissed, 'and I'm proud of it, and – and I'm going to make *you* one before I've finished with you!'

THE SECRET OF THE SERVICES

Pride of city, calling, class, and creed imposes standards and obligations which hold men above themselves at a pinch, and steady them through long strain. One meets it in the New Army at every turn, from the picked Territorials who slipped across Channel last night to the six-week-old Service battalion maturing itself in mud. It is balanced by the ineradicable English instinct to understate, detract, and decry – to mask the thing done by loudly drawing attention to the things undone. The more one sees of the camps the more one is filled with facts and figures of joyous significance, which will become clearer as the days lengthen; and the less one hears of the endurance, decency, self-sacrifice, and utter devotion which have made, and are hourly making, this wonderful new world. The camps take this for granted – else why should any man be there at all? He might have gone on with his business, or – watched 'soccer'. But having chosen to do his bit, he does it, and talks as much about his motives as he would of his religion or his love-affairs. He is eloquent over the shortcomings of the authorities, more pessimistic as to the future of his next neighbour battalion than would be safe to print, and lyric on his personal needs – baths and drying-rooms for choice. But when the grousing gets beyond a certain point – say at three a.m. in steady wet, with the tent-pegs drawing like false teeth – the nephew of the insurance-agent asks the cousin of the baronet to inquire of the son of the fried-fish vendor what the stevedore's brother and the tutor of the public school joined the Army *for*. Then they sing 'Somewhere the Sun is Shining' till the Sergeant Ironmonger's assistant cautions them to drown in silence or the Lieutenant telephone-appliances-manufacturer will speak to them in the morning.

The New armies have not yet evolved their typical private, N.C.O., and officer, though one can see them shaping. They are humorous because, for all our long faces, we are the only genuinely humorous race on earth; but they all know for true that there are no excuses in the Service. 'If there *were*,' said a three-month-old under-gardener-private to me, 'what 'ud become of Discipline?'

They are already setting standards for the coming millions, and have sown little sprouts of regimental tradition which may grow into age-old trees. In one corps, for example, though no dubbin is issued, a man loses his name for parading with dirty boots. He looks down scornfully on the next battalion where they are not expected to achieve the impossible. In another – an ex-Guards sergeant brought 'em up by hand – the drill is rather high-class. In a third they fuss about records for route-marching, and men who fall out have to explain themselves to their sweating companions. This is entirely right. They are all now in the Year One, and the meanest of them may be an ancestor of whom regimental posterity will say: 'There were giants in those days!'

The Real Question

This much we can realise, even though we are so close to it. The old safe instinct saves us from triumph and exultation. But what will be the position in years to come of the young man who has deliberately elected to outcaste himself from this all-embracing brotherhood? What of his family, and, above all, what of his descendants, when the books have been closed and the last balance struck of sacrifice and sorrow in every hamlet, village, parish, suburb, city, shire, district, province, and Dominion throughout the Empire?